When God Speaks through Change

The Vital Worship, Healthy Congregations Series

John D. Witvliet, Series Editor

Published by the Alban Institute in Cooperation with the
Calvin Institute of Christian Worship

BOOKS PUBLISHED

C. Michael Hawn
One Bread, One Body:
Exploring Cultural Diversity in Worship

Norma deWaal Malefyt and Howard Vanderwell
Designing Worship Together:
Models and Strategies for Worship Planning

Craig A. Satterlee
When God Speaks through Change:
Preaching in Times of Congregational Transition

Vital Worship, Healthy Congregations

When God Speaks through Change

PREACHING IN TIMES OF CONGREGATIONAL TRANSITION

Craig A. Satterlee

THE
ALBAN
INSTITUTE
Herndon, Virginia
www.alban.org

Bl. Alban ³/₀₅ [18.00]

The Alban Institute, 2121 Cooperative Way, Suite 100, Herndon, VA 20171

This material may not be photocopied or reproduced in any way without written permission. Go to www.alban.org/permissions.asp

Scripture quotations, unless otherwise noted, are from the New Revised Standard Version of the Bible, © 1989, Division of Christian Education of the National Council of Churches of Christ in the United States of America, and are used by permission.

Cover and text design by Keith McCormick.

Cover illustration by Tacoumba Aiken.

Library of Congress Cataloging-in-Publication Data

Satterlee, Craig Alan, 1959-
  When God speaks through change : preaching in times of congregational transition / Craig A. Satterlee.
      p. cm. — (Vital worship, healthy congregations)
  Includes bibliographical references.
  ISBN 1-56699-297-4
  1. Church renewal. 2. Change—Religious aspects—Christianity. I. Title. II. Series.

  BV600.3.S27 2005
  251—dc22
                          2004029273

        09 08 07 06 05   VG   1 2 3 4 5

For Chelsey Grace

CONTENTS

EDITOR'S FOREWORD

HEALTHY CONGREGATIONS

Christianity is a "first-person plural" religion, where communal worship, service, fellowship, and learning are indispensable for grounding and forming individual faith. The strength of Christianity in North America depends on the presence of healthy, spiritually nourishing, well-functioning congregations. Congregations are the cradle of Christian faith, the communities in which children of all ages are supported, encouraged, and formed for lives of service. Congregations are the habitat in which the practices of the Christian life can flourish.

As living organisms, congregations are by definition in a constant state of change. Whether the changes are in membership, pastoral leadership, lay leadership, the needs of the community, or the broader culture, a crucial mark of healthy congregations is their ability to deal creatively and positively with change. The fast pace of change in contemporary culture, with its bias toward, not against, change only makes the challenge of negotiating change all the more pressing for congregations.

VITAL WORSHIP

At the center of many discussions about change in churches today is the topic of worship. This is not surprising, for worship is at the center of congregational life. To "go to church" means, for most members of congregations, "to go to worship." In *How Do We Worship?*, Mark Chaves begins his analysis with the simple assertion, "Worship is the most central and public activity engaged in by American religious congregations" (Alban Institute, 1999, p. 1). Worship styles are one of the most significant reasons that people choose to join a given congregation. Correspondingly, they are central to the identity of most congregations.

Worship is also central on a much deeper level. Worship is the locus of what several Christian traditions identify as the nourishing center of congregation life: preaching, common prayer, and the celebration of ordinances or sacraments. Significantly, what many traditions elevate to the status of "the means of grace" or even the "marks of the church" are essentially liturgical actions. Worship is central, most significantly, for theological reasons. Worship both reflects and shapes a community's faith. It expresses a congregation's view of God and enacts a congregation's relationship with God and each other.

We can identify several specific factors that contribute to spiritually vital worship and thereby strengthen congregational life.

- Congregations, and the leaders that serve them, need a shared vision for worship that is grounded in more than personal aesthetic tastes. This vision must draw on the deep theological resources of Scripture, the Christian tradition, and the unique history of the congregation.
- Congregational worship should be integrated with the whole life of the congregation. It can serve as the "source and summit" from which all the practices of the Christian life flow. Worship both reflects and shapes the life of the church in education, pastoral care, community service, fellowship, justice, hospitality, and every other aspect of church life.
- The best worship practices feature not only good worship "content," such as discerning sermons, honest prayers, creative artistic contributions, celebrative and meaningful rituals for baptism and the Lord's Supper. They also arise of out of good process, involving meaningful contributions from participants, thoughtful leadership, honest evaluation, and healthy communication among leaders.

VITAL WORSHIP, HEALTHY CONGREGATIONS SERIES

The Vital Worship, Healthy Congregations Series is designed to reflect the kind of vibrant, creative energy and patient reflection that will promote worship that is both relevant and profound. It is designed to invite congregations to rediscover a common vision for worship, to sense how worship is related to all aspects of congregational life, and to imagine better ways of preparing both better "content" and better "process" related to the worship life of their own congregations.

It is important to note that strengthening congregational life through worship renewal is a delicate and challenging task precisely because of the uniqueness of each congregation. This book series is not designed to represent a single denomination, Christian tradition, or type of congregation. Nor is it designed to serve as arbiter of theological disputes about worship. Books in the series will note the significance of theological claims about worship, but they may, in fact, represent quite different theological visions from each other, or from our work at the Calvin Institute of Christian Worship. That is, the series is designed to call attention to instructive examples of congregational life and to explore these examples in ways that allow readers in very different communities to compare and contrast these examples with their own practice. The models described in any given book may for some readers be instructive as examples to follow. For others, a given example may remind them of something they are already doing well, or something they will choose not to follow because of theological commitments or community history.

In the first volume in our series, *One Bread, One Body: Exploring Cultural Diversity in Worship*, Michael Hawn posed the poignant question "is there room for my neighbor at the table?" and explored what four multicultural congregations have to teach us about hospitality and the virtues of cross-cultural worship. His work helps us step back and reflect on the core identity of our congregations.

In our second volume, *Designing Worship Together: Models and Strategies for Worship Planning*, Norma deWaal Malefyt and Howard Vanderwell enter the trenches of weekly congregational life. They give us helpful insights into the process of how services are planned and led. It is hard to overstate the significance of this topic. For without a thoughtful, discerning, collaborative worship planning process, all manner of worship books, conferences, and renewal programs are likely either to make no inroads into the life of a given congregation or, when they do, to damage rather than renew congregational life.

In this third volume, *When God Speaks through Change: Preaching in Times of Congregational Transition,* Craig Satterlee addresses the question of how worship (and particularly preaching) might best respond to times of significant congregational transition. The vast majority of published perspectives and resources for preaching and worship unwittingly assume a level of constancy in congregational life, taking for granted that the congregation will have the resources (emotional and otherwise) to absorb some significant new message or practice. However, on any given Sunday, a strikingly large number of churches are simply trying to cope with a significant transition in community life or leadership. These transitions do limit what preachers and worship leaders can do on Sunday, but they also present unparalleled opportunities for the reception of the gospel. For congregations in transition, this book provides a useful and necessary frame for viewing almost all other advice and resources about what should happen in public worship.

By promoting encounters with instructive examples from various parts of the body of Christ, we pray that these volumes will help leaders make good judgments about worship in their congregations and that, by the power of God's Spirit, these congregations will flourish.

John D. Witvliet
Calvin Institute of Christian Worship

PREFACE

On Friday afternoon, Pastor Souris is sitting in her office, working on Sunday's sermon, when the telephone rings. The caller tells her that the major employer in the community has just announced layoffs. Some of the managers who make the decisions and some of those affected by the layoffs are members of the congregation.

In another community, a telephone call to Pastor Cromwell's home late Friday evening informs him that the congregation's church building is on fire, and he rushes to the church. As the evening progresses, it becomes obvious that the fire damage is serious enough that the congregation will not be able to worship in the building on Sunday.

In a third congregation, as Pastor Stuart spends the Saturday morning before confirmation Sunday reviewing his sermon, a police officer arrives at the church to ask some questions. It seems that the confirmation teacher, a beloved board member scheduled to assist in the service, has been charged with child sexual abuse. The accusation comes from a member of the confirmation class.

In yet another congregation, Pastor Perkins opens the mailbox and finds a letter from a lawyer, which states that a deceased member bequeathed the congregation $2 million.

In many congregations, the chair of the pulpit committee telephones the pastor of another congregation to invite him or her to come for an interview or to consider a change in call. In many more congregations, the pastor pauses from preparing the Sunday sermon to look out the window and note for the hundredth time that the people in the neighborhood are very different from the members of the church and that the congregation is not doing much to welcome them.

As these pastors return to preparing their sermons, something is different. Another voice is asking to be heard; another participant is demanding
to speak; another reality needs to be addressed. An event that will launch a
time of *congregational transition*—a process of reshaping the congregation's
faith foundation, identity, and ways of being—has found its way into the
preaching. As the preacher studies Scripture, the transition and the biblical
text seem to interpret each another. The preacher wonders how the transition will affect his or her ability to proclaim and the congregation's ability
to receive the message. As the congregation works its way through the transition, the pastor ponders how preaching and worship, the congregation's
essential activity, can collaborate with other congregational processes involved in the transition. Most important, the preacher weighs the benefits
and risks of using preaching to address the transition and ponders how to
incorporate the transition into the form, content, and delivery of the sermon so that the gospel rather than an agenda is preached.

Regardless of what the pastor decides, a congregational transition will
find its way into preaching. Contemporary homiletic theory understands
that preaching cannot be reduced to a sermon text or manuscript but is, in
fact, an event involving several active participants. Generally speaking, these
participants include the congregation, the preacher, Scripture, God, and
the occasion. For example, Fred Craddock, professor emeritus of preaching
and New Testament at the Candler School of Theology, Atlanta, asserts that
the preacher "works within an unusual network of trust and intimacy that
makes the separation of character from performance impossible" and that
a sermon "is to be located among a particular group of listeners as much as
with a particular speaker."[1] Whether the Bible simply provides historical
continuity with the ongoing life of the people of God or determines the
sermon's central message, governing image, and basic vocabulary, Scripture is nonetheless indispensable to preaching. Since Peter's sermon at Pentecost, the church has affirmed that God the Creator, Christ, or the Holy
Spirit is the principal actor in preaching.[2] Anyone who has preached at a
wedding and a funeral in the same week can attest to the power of the
occasion to shape the preaching event. Charles Campbell, associate professor of homiletics at Columbia Theological Seminary, argues convincingly
that "the powers and principalities"—the powers of death at work in the
world—also participate in and shape our understanding of preaching.[3]
While the congregation, preacher, Scripture, the occasion, God, and even

the powers and principalities all contribute to the preaching event, the role and importance that each participant plays varies in every sermon.

In the life of every congregation and preacher, a congregational transition at times looms so large in a preaching event that it becomes the lens through which Scripture is interpreted, the congregation is addressed, the preacher is heard, and God is experienced. I intend this book to be a companion for preaching in these times of congregational transition. If we understand congregational transitions as *kairos* moments in the life of the congregation, occasions of grace that mark a definite and perhaps definitive shift in the life trajectory of the community,[4] preaching's potential as an effective tool and a faithful response becomes obvious.

Yet, as in every preaching event, the faithfulness and effectiveness of preaching in a time of congregational transition is not automatic. During a congregational transition, faithful preaching ensures that the gospel—and not a program or agenda—is proclaimed and heard. Effective preaching leads the congregation to experience God's presence, grace, power, and direction amid the transition. Faithful and effective preaching illuminates the mystery inherent in the transition, rather than seeking to eliminate it, so that God provides orientation and direction as the congregation moves into what is still unknown. Faithful and effective preaching models and declares that God speaks through change. God speaks as the congregation moves toward transition. The change itself may be the way God speaks.

In times of congregational transition, faithful and effective preaching calls for five foundational commitments from the preacher. These commitments can be summarized thus:

1. Comprehension of the dynamics of the transitional process and theological reflection on transitions generally and the particular transition the congregation is experiencing.
2. Trust in the power, purpose, and place of preaching in the congregation's journey of transition.
3. Willingness to welcome the transition into the process of sermon preparation.
4. Holy and active listening to the congregation, the community, and the self.
5. God's presence, grace, power and direction anchor the preacher amid the transition and when preaching through it.

Understanding that both preaching and managing transition are highly contextual, I will not provide in this book a blueprint or recipe for preaching through specific transitions. Instead, this book is intended as a companion for those called to preach in times of congregational transition, a conversation partner that will help preachers prepare, reflect, and pray as they preach during a congregational transition. The first part of this volume is devoted to theological reflection, practical suggestions, and prayerful assurance for the five foundational commitments necessary for faithful and effective preaching in times of congregational transition.

In chapter 1, I review the dynamics of transition and reflect theologically upon this process. In chapter 2, I explore the benefits and the risks, the power and the danger of preaching in times of transition. I also consider the purpose of such preaching and its place in congregational life, most notably the congregation's worship, and other processes and activities aimed at helping the congregation journey through the transition. In chapter 3, I encourage preachers to welcome the transition as a participant in sermon preparation and consider strategies for doing so. In chapter 4, I consider the congregation, the community, and the person of the preacher as voices through which the transition speaks. In chapter 5, I attempt to help the preacher remain grounded in the gospel and spiritually centered amid the change of transition and while preaching through it.

The second section of the book considers the congregational transitions that result from eight specific changes or events:

1. The person who holds the pastoral office changes.
2. A new vision for mission.
3. Significant increase or decrease in the worship attendance or financial giving of the congregation's members.
4. Completion of the congregation's ministry (the end of a congregation's life).
5. A traumatic event in the life of the congregation, community, or nation.
6. Betrayal of trust (financial, sexual, etc.) within the congregation.
7. An event or issue that causes tension or opposition between church and society.
8. The eruption of factions within the congregation.

Using the Five Foundational Commitments as a guide for approaching each situation, I consider the nature of the transition and the ways one might understand it theologically, the role of preaching in the transitional process, what the preacher ought to listen for and be mindful of in sermon preparation and delivery, Scripture passages that may prove insightful, and ways preachers might remain connected to God and nurture their spiritual well-being.

This volume is a compendium of the collected wisdom of pastors who have led or are leading congregations through significant transitions and who faithfully and effectively welcome the congregational transition as a participant in their preaching. Through a grant from the Louisville Institute, a Lilly Endowment program for the study of American religion, pastors with significant experience in preaching in times of congregational transition came together to reflect on their experience and to offer insights, questions, and orientation. This collected wisdom was clarified and refined through two courses I taught, the first at the Lutheran School of Theology at Chicago and the second as part of the Doctor of Ministry in Preaching program of the Association of Chicago Theological Schools. In the first course, students reviewed relevant literature on specific changes and interviewed pastors with significant experience in congregational transitions. In the second course, I presented lectures based on chapters of this book to pastors dealing with significant transitions, who incorporated insights and suggestions into their own preaching. Finally, in an attempt to seek the widest possible theological, congregational, and cultural diversity, I identified and interviewed pastors with perspectives and experiences that the study was lacking. This volume is ultimately blessed by the insights and revisions of preachers representing the Anglican, Baptist, Evangelical Covenant, Lutheran, Methodist, Metropolitan Community, Pentecostal, Presbyterian, Reformed, and Roman Catholic traditions of Christianity, as well as Reform Judaism. These women and men range in age from gen Xers to the World War II generation. They serve throughout North America and in Europe in a variety of contexts, bringing the perspectives of African American, Asian, European American, and Latino/a communities of faith. I am grateful to these committed leaders for generously offering their questions and convictions, encouragement and challenge, inspiration and insight. More important, I am grateful to God for the hopeful and faithful leadership that these preachers offer both their communities and our world.

I want to thank publicly the Louisville Institute for making possible the consultation on which this book is based, and for gracing me with an extended period to write by awarding a General Grant for this project. The Lutheran School of Theology at Chicago, where I am privileged to teach, provided gracious hospitality and logistical support to the consultation and welcomed this conversation into its curriculum. The Doctor of Ministry in Preaching program of the Association of Chicago Theological Schools and the Word in Worship Seminar of the North American Academy of Liturgy both proved to be important arenas in which to try out and refine ideas. Margaret and Tim Schoewe provided a beautiful and quiet sanctuary that invited creative thinking and writing.

One of the greatest joys of this project is that it is the confluence of teaching and research. In particular, the second section of this book is greatly indebted to the investigation, writing, and preaching of a cadre of my students, including Jen Beamsley (new vision), Micah Jackson (church and society in opposition), Carrie Lewis (pastoral transition), Jennifer Moland-Kovash (betrayal of trust), Peg Otte (trauma), and Benjamin Sandin (completion of ministry). I am grateful to Trish Madden, my student assistant, whose organizational skills, good humor, and attention to detail facilitate research and free me for reflection and writing. Trish's careful reading of and collaborative reflection on drafts of this manuscript make it a better work. Special thanks go to my colleague Connie Kleingartner, who saw the value of this project when it was scarcely an idea, and to John Witvliet and Beth Gaede, who helped to make the idea a reality. I am especially grateful for Beth's partnership, support, and expertise in working with pastors, as well as for her editorial skill.

As we dare to preach in times of congregational transition, we must come to terms with God's place and role in change. As a preacher and teacher, I have been privileged to witness God speaking through change, speaking grace and power that transformed both the congregations I have served and the students I teach. Yet, that God speaks through change is nowhere more evident to me than in the life of our daughter, Chelsey Grace. As my wife, Cathy, and I accompany Chelsey through the challenge and delight of each transition in her life, we are moved to praise the God of change. With gratitude to God, this book is therefore dedicated to Chelsey.

PART I

FOUNDATIONAL COMMITMENTS

In the best of all worlds, you are reading this book as you watch a pattern of change begin to form on your congregation's radar screen, and plenty of time remains to prepare for the brewing storm. It is far more likely that you opened this book because, like the preachers we met in the preface, you have heard a not-too-distant clap of thunder or may even find yourself caught in a downpour.

It may seem pragmatic to flip to the second part of this volume, scan the pertinent pages on the change and transition that your congregation faces, and formulate some first steps for a quick response. Pastors experienced with congregational transitions, however, caution us not to move too quickly. While a quick-fix, how-to approach may provide temporary stability, in the long term this approach is like building a house on sand: "The rain fell, and the floods came, and the winds blew and beat against that house, and it fell—and great was its fall!" (Matt. 7:27).

Congregational transitions require a solid foundation so that when the rain falls, the floods come, and the winds blow and beat on that house, the house does not fall, because it is founded on rock (Matt. 7:25).

These chapters describe the stones a preacher uses to build a foundation for preaching in times of congregational transition. They are commitments the preacher makes to understand the journey of transition, to trust preaching, to welcome the transition's participation in sermon preparation, to engage in holy and active listening, and to anchor oneself in God. Perhaps these "stones" seem obvious. Please take them in your hands and lay them in your ministry before you set out to build. The rain, the floods, and the wind can be strong.

CHAPTER 1

UNDERSTANDING THE JOURNEY OF TRANSITION

Were we to join the pastors we met in the preface in considering the situations that confront their congregations, we might be tempted to use Sunday's sermon to respond immediately to the situation in the hope of restoring a sense of normality. Pastor Souris might decide that Sunday's sermon will not take sides as labor and management work through layoffs. Pastor Cromwell might choose to begin Sunday's sermon by proclaiming that the congregation will rebuild after the fire. Pastor Stuart might announce that the accused confirmation teacher will not be permitted to participate in the service. Pastor Perkins might announce the bequest with the caveat that the congregation will give 10 percent away. Despite clear responses like these, the congregation does not return to the life it considered normal.

As we decide how to preach in times of congregational transition, executive development consultant William Bridges offers advice to business mangers in his national best seller *Managing Transitions: Making the Most of Change* that is equally valuable to preachers: it is essential to distinguish between change and transition.[1] *Change* is situational. Situations arise that change the congregation. The largest employer in town announces layoffs. The congregation no longer reflects the neighborhood surrounding the church building. The congregation unexpectedly receives $2 million. A congregation's success at responding to any change ultimately depends upon the congregation's claiming a new identity and adopting new ways of being in response to the new situation. When congregations fail to claim new identities and adopt new ways of being in response to change, ministries stall and become less relevant; congregational life deteriorates.

Congregational transition is the process of reshaping the congregation's faith foundation, identity, and ways of being in response to change that results from a new situation. Whereas change is situational, transition is a psychological journey from the congregation's established identity to the identity befitting the reality brought on by change. Transition is the process by which a congregation comes to terms with layoffs in its community, adapts or fails to adapt to its changing neighborhood, or determines how it will minister as a faith community with considerable financial resources. All congregations experience changes that alter their faith foundation, identity, and ways of being. How congregations manage the transitions determines the character of their life and ministry in the new reality.

When a congregation confuses change and transition, it is concerned with the outcome that the change produces and the task of resolving that outcome. For example, a congregation that cannot meet its budget may assess all its ministries in terms of its financial "bottom line" to solve the problem. Unfortunately, when a congregation approaches change in this manner, the situation becomes more complicated as the congregation's spirit, energy, and ability to function diminish. On the other hand, when a congregation approaches a change as *initiating* a transition, the congregation itself becomes the focus. The starting point in a transition is not finding the solution to the problem. The starting point is identifying what the congregation needs to let go of, the ending that the congregation needs to make. The budget deficit serves as an indication that the congregation needs to let go of things as they are to renew its mission and relationship to the community it serves. It is only by making this ending that the congregation can move into the new reality brought on by the change. Adapting to this new reality is a process in which the congregation embraces the change in such a way that it can let go of an old identity and reality to become something new.

TRANSITIONS BEGIN WITH CHANGE

Today congregations are confronted by many kinds of changes that move them into transition. In a fascinating study of our changing world, priest and social psychologist Diarmuid O'Murchú argues that as a species, human beings are in an age of transition—the old securities are gone, and the new possibilities are still ambiguous.[2] O'Murchú explores the nature of this transition in some of its more obvious manifestations. O'Murchú calls these manifestations the move from mechanistic to wholistic paradigms, from a static to a dynamic worldview, from closed to open systems, from classical to quantum science, and from simplified to integrated spirituality. O'Murchú demonstrates that human interactions have shifted from independence to interdependence. Institutional structures have evolved into networks. In O'Murchú's terms, thinking has gone from linear to lateral; that is, from using information sequentially to solve problems to using information creatively to consider challenges that will (in all likelihood) open up new possibilities for perceiving and understanding reality. The pendulum of authority is swinging from masculine to feminine. Rather than being church-centered, theology is now kingdom-centered. Evolution is no longer physical but psychic.

Within congregational life, the changes brought on by a postmodern world, a post-Christian culture, and a postdenominational church have caused profound transitions in theological understanding, doctrine, Christian practice, and the church's place in society—so profound that many pastors regard change as a normal and expected part of parish ministry. In our postmodern world, congregations are challenged by an American culture that increasingly values experience over authority, ambiguities over absolutes, and meaning derived from many stories, rather than from a single narrative. Despite the assumptions held by many congregations, the diverse forms of religion, competing value systems, and privatized Christianity that characterize contemporary society reveal that if American culture was ever truly "Christian," that time has passed. Finally, although denominational labels once defined congregational life, today people's decisions to join faith communities are based on how well their spiritual needs are met.

The changes encapsulated by the terms postmodernity, post-Christendom, and postdenominationalism compel Christian leaders increasingly to conclude that congregational life, like life itself, is not stable. Rather than anticipating, preparing for, and responding to the change that will initiate a congregational transition, as if that change were an isolated event, these pastors understand all ministry as transitional. For them, congregational life is an ongoing process composed of overlapping transitions. Instead of initiating transitions, the acute changes or crises in the life of a congregation alter the pace and intensity of ongoing transition. From this

perspective, the first task in leading congregations in transition is not anticipating the next change but sorting through and identifying the changes
continually occurring in the congregation's life.

Joseph Jeter, professor of homiletics at Brite Divinity School, at Texas
Christian University, asserts that three types of crises tend to interrupt an
orderly homiletic agenda: public, congregational, and personal.[3] Public crises include political crises and natural and other kinds of disasters. Congregational crises affect a particular local church. Personal crises strike
directly at members of the congregation, people in the community, and
even the preacher. All three types of change have the potential to launch a
congregational transition.

We might further distinguish changes that cause congregational transitions by whether they originate outside or within the congregation. For
example, the process of creating and embracing a new vision for mission is
generally a transition initiated by the congregation itself. We might also
consider the nature of the change. Some changes are unexpected and unin-
vited; others are planned for, anticipated, and welcomed. While change can
be traumatic with obvious long-term consequences, it can also be slow and
subtle with hidden implications. Finally, the changes that bring on congregational transition are both unpredictable and part of a congregation's natural development. These changes may be temporary or permanent.

In and of itself, change is neutral. Any change can be approached as
either a threat or an opportunity, either a cause for celebration or a reason
to despair. The issue confronting congregations and their leaders is not the
changes themselves. The issue is the congregation's response to both the
change and the transition it initiates. Generally, people instinctively resist
transitions for two reasons. First, people naturally struggle to protect their
world and the meaning and identity they receive through it. Even a positive
change threatens that world of meaning and identity. In many congregations, denial is a favorite form of resistance. To address people's resistance
to change, leaders need to address the threat to people's world of meaning
posed by the change.

The second reason congregations resist transition is that, ideally, they
do not want to enter into a new world of meaning and identity until everyone is comfortable with it. At its best, the congregation's desire to resist
until everyone is on board is rooted in its desire to maintain the commu-

nity, to avoid additional conflict, and to value all members of the congregation. Resistance is a way of giving people time to become at ease with the
new reality. Unfortunately, change comes so fast today in every area of life
that people are given less and less time to get comfortable. In fact, in many
areas of congregational life, transition and the new world of meaning and
identity that it brings cannot be delayed until everyone is on board. This
pressure to move quickly is particularly difficult because many people rely
on their congregation to be a place of permanence and stability in an ever-
changing world. Many communities of faith also go to great lengths both to
honor every opinion and to avoid the conflict that may result from moving
in any direction with less than complete consensus. To help the congregation embrace the transition, leaders must make it their priority to help people
understand and "own" problems brought on by the change as important,
urgent, and solvable before attempting to initiate and implement solutions.
The trek from understanding and owning the problem to initiating and
implementing a solution is one way of envisioning a congregational transition; the dynamics of transition make for a long and difficult trip. Bringing
the congregation through the transition that results from change is essential to its faith, community, mission, and life as the members find themselves in a new reality.

THE DYNAMICS OF TRANSITION

William Bridges defines *transition* as a three-phase process that people go
through as they internalize and come to terms with the new situation that
a change brings about.[4] Bridges labels these three phases "Ending," "Neutral Zone," and "New Beginning." Bridges uses the word *phases* to describe
these three elements, possibly giving the impression that they are stages,
periods of time, or chapters in a book. Leaders of congregational transition make clear that Bridges's model is helpful for understanding congregational transitions when the three parts—Ending, Neutral Zone, and
New Beginning—are understood not as phases, but as threads or strands
woven into the tapestry of the congregation's life. In this section, we will
examine each strand in turn and conclude by suggesting ways leaders might
nuance this model to comprehend more fully the dynamics of congregational transition.

Ending

In every transition, things end. Congregations must let go of at least part of their old identity and ways of doing things—even when changes are welcomed. For example, when a mission congregation moves into its own church building, it must give up both its nomadic identity and its practice of unpacking before worship and packing up afterward. Letting go is made more difficult because the things the congregation must relinquish are often the very things that got the congregation where it is. When it reaches a certain size, a congregation that understands itself as a "close-knit family" must let go of and change its identity if it is to continue to grow. The problem, of course, is that people do not like endings and the losses that they bring. Therefore, the primary task in dealing with this strand of transition is to help people deal with their losses and to counter their denial. People who drag their feet, resist, and undermine have good and valid reasons for doing so, at least from their perspective. Ending requires that leaders discover what those reasons are and address them.

Liminal Strand

While Bridges labels the second phase of transition the Neutral Zone, I prefer to call it the liminal strand.[5] From the Latin *limen,* or threshold, this liminal strand is an in-between time when the old is gone but the new has not fully arrived. The liminal phase takes place in time, space, or both time and space, and can last months or even years. During this time, people experience partial, if not complete, separation from established roles, status, and behavior. Since old structures are passing away and new structures are not yet established, people develop structures unique to the liminal phrase and use them to deconstruct and reconstruct identity and ways of being and doing, so that the critical psychological realignments and repatternings take place in both individuals and the corporate culture. The provisional and temporary nature of liminality leads many researchers to liken it to death, to being in the womb; to invisibility, darkness, the wilderness, and an eclipse of the moon or sun.[6]

Yet liminality is not the wasted and meaningless time that it often seems to be. The liminal strand of transition is a time of reorientation and redirection. The deconstruction and reconstruction of established ways of doing and being can renew motivation and give people space to take new initiatives that result in inspired words and actions. Questions can lead to breakthrough answers. Chaos is more hospitable to new ideas than are standardized methods and routines.

The problem inherent in this strand of transition is that separation from established roles, status, and behavior causes people's anxiety to rise and their motivation to fall. They tend to withdraw, becoming less regular in worship and less active in congregational life. Old wounds in the congregation's history reopen, and old weaknesses reemerge. People are overloaded. They may become polarized. The congregation becomes vulnerable even to attack from outside, as when neighboring congregations begin to look healthier and more attractive. Feeling the danger inherent in this strand of transition, the members are tempted to rush through or to act out of fear. Approached as an opportune time, the liminal strand has the potential to be the most creative time in the transition.

Congregational leaders undertake three tasks to make the liminal strand a creative opportunity rather than a frightening wasteland:

1. Provide enough order to get people through in one piece.
2. Capitalize simultaneously on the confusion of the liminal strand by encouraging innovation, promoting experimentation, seeking new solutions to old problems, and embracing failures as valuable.
3. Resist the desire for certainty and closure. Congregations often try too quickly to "get back to normal" when in reality there is no "normal" to get back to. Resisting people's desire for certainty and closure is continuous.

New Beginning

The third strand in the transitional process is a new beginning. This is the time when the congregation develops its new identity, experiences new energy, and discovers the new direction and sense of purpose that enable it to live into its new reality. New beginnings are characterized by new understandings, new attitudes, new values, new identities, or a combination of any of these. The challenge inherent in this strand of transition is that people want new beginnings to happen but at the same time fear them. New beginnings trigger old anxieties and involve risk. They force people to come to terms with both the possibility of failure and the impossibility of return-ing to the way things were; this recognition may conjure up a sense of nos-talgia that has the potential to stall or derail the new beginning. Finally, new beginnings are frightening because they conclude what was for some a pleas-ant experience—the spontaneity and chaos of the liminal strand.

Congregations cannot assume that new beginnings will happen auto-matically. In fact, congregational transitions often lack resolution, both in the congregation and in the heart and life of the preacher, even years later. For example, the circumstances surrounding a pastor's decision to leave a congregation may cause both the pastor and the congregation to second-guess long after the decision is made. Similarly, congregations that do not arrive at the new beginnings they hoped and planned for may never under-stand why. Since new beginnings are not automatic, a step-by-step plan is required for phasing in the new reality. This plan needs to be carefully de-signed and implemented; it must be well nurtured as it unfolds. Successful plans for implementing new beginnings include at least three components.

First, it is essential to explain the basic purpose for the new beginning that the congregation seeks. The purpose must be real, not vague or make-believe. Initiating a new beginning to be a "faithful," "missional," "vital," or "growing" congregation is too indefinite. Increasing membership by 200 people in the next two months is probably unrealistic. To be both possible and concrete, the purpose for a new beginning must grow out of the congregation's will, abilities, and resources, and from the way these charac-teristics interact with the congregation's present situation.

The second component of a successful plan for phasing in a new begin-ning is the creation of a picture, or image, of how the congregation will look and feel in the new reality. The picture in people's heads is the reality in which they live. Images therefore have the power to effect deep change in people, lift them into truth, and move them beyond themselves.[7] Fred Craddock argues that for the creation of a new identity and new behavior, images must be replaced, and this can be done only gradually, by other images.[8] Even before new images are established in people's minds, they change identity and behavior by challenging established images that are in reality inadequate, inaccurate, or incomplete. In addition to addressing people individually, a picture of the new beginning has the power to create a community with a shared vision. Walter Brueggemann, professor emeri-tus of Old Testament at Columbia Theological Seminary, Decatur, Georgia, reminds us of the power of images to move us outward (beyond the world that we know) by embodying an alternative vision of reality and giving us another world to enter.[9] In determining the picture of the new beginning, we must take care not to overwhelm people with an image that is intimidating rather than exciting.

The third component in a successful plan for making a new beginning is inviting participation. When planning new beginnings, provide as many members of the congregation as possible roles in both the plan and the new reality. Giving people something to do reassures them that they continue to be important, that they have a place in the new beginning, and that they will not be forgotten, left behind, or excluded. It is particularly important in making a new beginning to invite people who lost something significant in the transition and people who will lose something significant in the new reality to participate in both the journey of transition and the emerging reality. Leaders must do more than tell the congregation why the transition is necessary. Leaders need to involve as many people as possible in the transition to give members more convincing, firsthand experience of the problems that make letting go and beginning anew necessary. For example, the transition toward building expansion, necessitated by an overcrowded Sunday school, is much more palatable to those who have spent time teaching. Involving as many people as possible in the new beginning also makes the congregation and its leaders allies rather than adversaries, and helps everyone to become invested in the success of the new beginning.

Limits of the Model

While Bridges's model is helpful for understanding congregational transitions, it is, like all models, limited in some significant ways.

First, rather than simply following a three-step process, congregational transitions are complex and multilayered events. Analyzing congregational transitions is more like looking through a kaleidoscope than at a series of slides. However desperately congregations may want a map to guide them, rarely do they find landmarks on the journey of transition that signal the end of one phase and the beginning of another. Sometimes a congregation's choices and decisions make it difficult to find the ending or new beginning. Rather than an easily defined procedure, transition is an ongoing journey in which endings, liminal phases, and beginnings all blend into one another and occur simultaneously in different areas of the congregation's life. This is why the consultants and I speak of the parts of transition as strands rather than steps.

Second, a congregational transition is rarely an isolated occurrence. Generally, one congregational transition brings on more transitions. When a pastor leaves, a congregation often reconsiders its mission, finances, and organizational plan. Congregational transitions can also initiate personal transitions in both the pastor and other leaders, congregational groups, and individuals in the congregation. Completing one transition may initiate another. When congregations experience multiple transitions, whether simultaneously or over time, "transition fatigue" is an essential but often overlooked factor that needs to be addressed by leaders. *Transition fatigue* describes the weariness and resistance that often result from the piling up of many transitions.

Third, congregational transitions are unpredictable. A transition may turn out to have an impact far beyond what we expect. Sometimes what a congregation *thinks of* as the transition turns out not to be the *real* transition. The course and direction of a transition can change quickly. People's perceptions and reactions rarely remain stable over time. Attentive listening to the congregation, flexibility, and a willingness to amend the transitional plan are therefore essential ingredients for successfully leading a congregation through transition.

Fourth, congregational transition involves more than abstract cognition and emotions. Congregational transitions generally have concrete dimensions that can be measured in time and space. S. Patrick Scully, a Marist priest, reminds us that the transitions made by Mexican immigrant communities cannot be approached as an abstract intellectual model or a mere mental sieve through which all people must pass, time and again, ad infinitum. In many Mexican communities, transition cannot be reduced to cognitive movements or moments of ambiguous grief, pain, hope, reconciliation, uncertainty, and disorientation because, for these communities, transitions have concrete, physically felt implications. For example, the Mexican immigrant may never see, touch, and embrace family members or friends ever again.[10] Particularly in contexts like this one, leading congregations in transition requires paying attention to such physical concerns as geography, congregational space, and the physical health and well-being of those making the transition.

Finally, congregational transitions always affect people's relationship with God. In every transition, congregations consider God's nature, purpose, and participation in light of the prevailing situation. Is God an anchor or a breeze? Is God comforting, challenging, punishing, or abandoning the congregation? What is God calling the congregation to do and to be? This situation and this transition—why are they happening? What is God's purpose, or is there no reason at all? To help congregations come to terms with these questions, preachers need to consider how they and their congregations might reflect theologically on the journey of transition.

THEOLOGICAL REFLECTION ON TRANSITION

In times of transition, our notions of God's nature, God's future, and our role in that future are often threatened. Those who dare to preach and to lead in times of congregational transition must themselves come to terms with God's place and role in change. Reflecting theologically on transition leads us to ask such questions as, Who does God show Godself to be in the midst of transition? Does God cause change, protect us from change, or empower us to respond to change? How do we, amid change, let God be God for the congregation and for the pastor? How do we know if a given change and transition are of God? How can we be certain of God's will and direction for us?

Ronald J. Allen, professor of preaching and New Testament at Christian Theological Seminary, Indianapolis, suggests that from a theological perspective, change and transition cause people of faith to experience two types of crises: *crises of understanding* and *crises of decision*.[11] Crises of understanding occur when people question the existence, identity, and nature of God. Confronted by a crisis of understanding, people often find themselves lost in a spiraling stream of consciousness in which one unanswered question leads to another. For example, people may ask:

> Is God all-knowing, all-powerful, and all-loving? If so, how could this crisis have happened? Since this did happen, what does that say about God's nature? Could God have intervened to minimize or even prevent this? Could we have done something to persuade God to intervene? Do we know what that is? Why would God need to be persuaded? If God could intervene, why didn't God intervene? If we could do something to persuade God to intervene, why didn't we?

People question God's will in the crisis. They also question God's existence. When God does not seem to act in the way people expect, they often
question the truth of God's very existence.

Crises of decision arise when people do not know how to respond when
they are unavoidably confronted by a given situation or issue. These situations and issues escalate into crises of decision when people do not have
time to consider their response, when the way they want to respond differs
from the way they know or are told they should respond, or when they are
confronted with circumstances unlike anything they have previously encountered and have no precedent to guide them.

Although we have discussed crises of understanding and crises of decision separately, Allen reminds us that they are inseparably linked. Our understanding of God influences and may even determine how we respond to
crisis, change, and transition. We respond one way if we trust a God who is
with us in suffering, bringing life out of death and light out of darkness. We
respond another way if we are convinced that God is distant, indifferent, or
even dead. We respond a third way if we conclude that the crisis, change, or
transition is the result of divine activity and judgment. From a theological
perspective, how we decide to respond to change, crisis, and transition is
shaped, if not determined, by our understanding of God. On some level, a
crisis of decision results from a crisis of understanding. If our basic understanding of God as faithful, loving, and present remains unshaken by change
and transition, we will be able to discern and decide how to respond. At the
same time, we recognize that change and transition will nuance, refine, challenge, and enrich this foundational understanding of God.

Speak of the Transition Biblically

As we attempt to respond to crises of understanding and decision, telling
the story of the congregation's transition by means of biblical images and
narratives helps to connect the transition to God's ongoing work of salvation. The stories of the Bible declare that God's work of salvation is transitional, involving an ending, an in-between time, and a new beginning. God's
leading Israel out of slavery in Egypt through the wilderness into the land
of promise is perhaps the most obvious example. Paul's journey from Jerusalem to Damascus is another. Jonah's time in the belly of the fish is an in-
between phase that marked an ending and a new beginning in Jonah's

ministry, as is Jesus' encounter with a Canaanite woman from the region of Tyre and Sidon (Matt. 15:21-28).

The choice of biblical stories and images that connect with a particular transition is immense and suggests many ways of approaching both Scripture and the congregational transition. Leaders and congregations in transition that read the Bible through the lens of transition, and approach the transition trusting the God revealed in Scripture, inevitably discover new insights, perspectives, and possibilities for moving forward. Preachers and congregations might begin by turning to the lectionary and their favorite Bible stories. Then, recognizing that both congregations and faith traditions have cherished Bible stories and images, we all need to expand our use of biblical story and image to gain even greater insight. For when we read the Bible through the lens of transition, allowing Scripture to shape our understanding as well as our response, both our favorite stories and many others reveal a God who continually transforms the world, a God who will not quit on us until the whole world is restored to the life God intends.

Using the language of the Bible to speak of and reflect on the congregation's transition also helps the preacher and congregation to realize that, as the people of God, they are by faith and calling a transitional people. Experiencing change, receiving new insight and understanding, and embracing a new call and direction are all normal and expected parts of the life of faith. Of course, understanding themselves as transitional people can make congregations and their leaders suspicious of God because each transition is experienced as preparation for another. In such situations, it is helpful for congregations and their leaders to reflect on the congregation's history to rediscover that God has always provided for the congregation. Faith communities have hope because they have seen how God provides. They are also reminded that, as God's people, we do not need to find God in transition; God always finds us. Even the prophet Elijah, who in a time of crisis went looking for God, did not find God in earthquake, wind, and fire. Instead, God found Elijah in a still small voice (1 Kings 19:1-18).

As a congregation seeks to discern God's will, speaking biblically of the transition also reveals that, from Israel's transition through the wilderness to Jesus' transition by way of the cross, God's way is usually the more difficult option. Congregations may find that the most faithful way to engage the transition is also the more difficult one. A declining congregation may decide to forgo the struggle to regain viability and instead choose the more

difficult path of completing its ministry as a tangible witness to the new life
that God will bring out of the congregation's death. Today, the church increasingly hears the call to respond to betrayals of trust by church leaders
by choosing the more difficult path of openness and candor.

Homiletical Reflections on Transition

Reflecting biblically on the change and transition confronting our church
and the world, contemporary homileticians offer theological perspectives
helpful to congregations and preachers pondering change and transition. I
offer brief summaries of a sampling of their work both for the insights they
offer and as examples of how preachers might use Scripture to reflect upon
congregational transition.

In *Cadences of Home: Preaching Among Exiles,* Walter Brueggemann
suggests that *exile*—together with the Old Testament experience of and reflection upon it—is a helpful *metaphor* for understanding the current faith
situation in the church in the United States. As a metaphor, exile has "an
odd, playful, ill-fitting match to its reality, the purpose of which is to illuminate and evoke dimensions of reality which will go unnoticed and therefore unexperienced."[12] Displacement, failed hopes, anger, wistful sadness,
and helplessness penetrate our sense of self, sense of community, and sense
of future. Brueggemann proposes that our posture for preaching is as an
exile addressing exiles. We are helped in our preaching by pondering the
interface of our experience of the circumstances of exile with the scriptural
resources that grow from and address the faith crisis of exile. Such pondering reveals that exile need not lead us "to abandon faith, or to settle for
abdicating despair, nor to retreat to privatistic religion." The biblical response to exile is grounded in a sense and sureness that God is doing something new that circumstances cannot undermine or negate.

Joseph Jeter invites preachers to reflect on crises and the transitions
they initiate as a pilgrimage that calls the congregation out of its everyday
life in quest for God.[13] Congregations must learn both the patterns of pilgrimage and the customs and rules of the road. They must discover and
differentiate between what is stable and what is subject to change, what is
essential and what must be left behind. Pilgrims negotiate roadblocks, see a
familiar landscape change, and even change a familiar landscape themselves.
They uncover and discover what they initially overlooked. Pilgrims watch

for signs of danger and listen to guides who both warn and recommend. Most important, pilgrims reflect upon the goal of their journey, where they are headed, and why they are setting out. Preaching can assure listeners that God is on the road with them. Preaching can also help the congregation determine if it should continue on the same road, take a different path, turn around and go back the way it came, run to secure places of God's safety and stability, venture out into the unknown, or stop, be still, and wait.

Thomas H. Troeger, professor of preaching and communication at Iliff School of Theology, in Denver, invites us to see the church as an edifice of thought and belief that is marked by an unmistakable incompleteness. The church's walls are still standing and its space remains defined, but there is a hole in the ceiling above the altar where a mosaic of the Almighty used to be. This "God-shaped hole" serves as Troeger's poetic expression of the church's loss of commanding certitude about God. Preachers are challenged to bear witness to God with an imaginative power that vitalizes faith and ministry as Christians and congregations reconstruct their understanding of belief, worship, and ministry.[14] To do this, preachers must open themselves up to Scripture as the "visions and voices of the cloud of witnesses (Heb. 11:1–12:1) borne by the wind of the Spirit that will guide us 'into all the truth' (John 16:13)."[15] These witnesses remind us that ours is not the first age in which the church's dome of meaning has collapsed; whenever this happened, the Spirit stirred God's people to a more expansive understanding of God. That new image dominated the church's dome of meaning until it also crumbled and the Sprit blew yet again. Thus, for Troeger, the Bible canonizes a process of perpetually revising our theologies. Troeger cautions that we must expect inherited interpretation to be in tension with experience. This tension is rooted in God, who is not confined to the Bible and the past. Troeger writes, "We have a technical term for people who do not change: dead. If Christ has not changed since the resurrection, then Christ is no longer alive."[16] This process of theological reconstruction brings sorrow because it means acknowledging the loss of things once held sacred. To follow Troeger's metaphor: though the Spirit provides a new, more expansive image of God to replace the cherished image of God that is crumbling, this new image of God, which brings the church's resurrection, is terrifying before it is empowering because resurrection gives more freedom to Christ than most believers want their Savior to have.[17]

Finally, Charles Campbell's book *The Word Before the Powers* provides theological insight into resistance in transition. Bridges's model of transition suggests that people's resistance in a transition can be traced to fear, sense of loss, lack of understanding, or lack of ownership. Bridges makes the case that leaders overcome resistance by discovering the reasons people resist and addressing them. As I said in the preface, however, Campbell's work suggests that, more than the consequence of the psychological state of the congregation or the incompetence or mismanagement of its leaders, resistance in transitions and in preaching may be due in part to the participation of the powers and principalities—that is, the powers of death at work in the world. Campbell argues that the world's powers and principalities act aggressively in subtle but deadly ways that shape human life today and provide the context for Christian preaching.[18] The New Testament writers capture a sense of the multiplicity and omnipresence of these powers, which impinge on human life from every conceivable angle. The powers work through concrete, material institutions, structures, and systems—including congregations—to rebel against God by making idols of themselves and placing their own desires above God's purposes for humanity and creation. The powers use such tactics as negative sanctions, rewards and promises, isolation and division, demoralization and diversion, surveillance and secrecy, language and image to secure their own survival, dominate humanity, and bring chaos to the world. Campbell presents preaching the Word of God as a critical act of nonviolent resistance to the work of these destructive powers. Preaching as an act of nonviolent resistance is central to both Jesus' own preaching and our proclamation of Jesus' life, death, and resurrection. Finally, Campbell suggests that congregations are in continual transition when they seek to engage the powers as communities of resistance shaped by a distinctive worldview and by specific practices and virtues.

We will hear more from these and other colleagues in the next chapter as we consider the purpose and place of preaching in times of congregational transition. For now, they provide examples and insights as we reflect theologically on the transitional process and affirm God's presence, power, and purpose as congregations journey through it. Assured that God is with us on this journey, speaking through change, we are bold to preach through congregational transitions.

Questions for Reflection

- Do you consider the very nature of your congregation's life and your ministry to be transitional? Why or why not?
- Name a transition that is occurring in your congregation. What change(s) has your congregation experienced that initiated this transition?
- Identify evidence of each of the three strands of the transitional process that is occurring in your congregation—ending, liminal phase, new beginning.
- What biblical image or story would you use to describe your congregation's transition? What insights does this biblical image or story offer your understanding of the transition?

CHAPTER 2

TRUST PREACHING

It is the Friday or Saturday after an event such as a round of layoffs, a fire, an arrest, or an unexpected bequest launched a transition in the congregation. Staring at blank computer screens or empty legal pads, many pastors anxiously ask themselves, "*Should* I talk about this in the sermon? Would someone please tell me *how*?" Pastors experienced in leading congregations through transitions respond that preachers really do not have a choice; one way or another, the transition finds its way into the congregation's preaching ministry. The issue, then, is not *whether* the transition will be part of preaching and preaching part of the transition. Rather it is determining *how* preaching will participate in the transition and how the transition will participate in preaching. The answer depends, in part, on whether pastor and congregation trust preaching as a partner in leading congregational transition.

Caught in the chaos and confusion of transition and needing a support to hold on to, preachers may be tempted to answer the "how" question more concretely by rushing into the mechanics of crafting the "transitional sermon." After all, Sunday is just a day or two away. Pastors experienced in congregational transitions would invite us to slow down; they advise that deciding how to write the "transitional sermon" becomes much clearer when the preacher takes a deep breath, offers even a hurried prayer, and spends time asking, "How can I use preaching to make this transition easier? If I do preach about the transition, what precautions do I need to take?" By considering the ways preaching can both facilitate and complicate the congregational transition, preachers make the first and perhaps most important decision about preaching in times of congregational transition. They choose to trust preaching as a powerful ally in leading the congregation through transition. This chapter is devoted to examining the partnership of preaching and congregational transition. We will then turn to the practicalities of preparing and preaching the transitional sermon (chapter 3) and the holy and active listening that is fundamental to discovering what to say when preaching in times of congregational transition (chapter 4). I invite you to breathe, pray, and pause here before worrying about preparing that sermon. Trusting the bond between preaching and congregational transition will make preparation easier. Besides, my hunch is that at least a little time remains before Sunday.

PARTNERING IN PREACHING AND CONGREGATIONAL TRANSITION

At their best, preaching and other tasks required to lead the transition complement each other rather than ignoring or undermining each other. If preaching and leading the transition are to form this partnership, the pastor, at least, needs to acknowledge the transition, and both the congregation and its pastor must trust preaching. To "trust preaching" is to embrace the sermon as a word from the Lord. To trust preaching is to dare to believe that God speaks in and through preaching, particularly amid change, and that what the congregation hears and experiences is the power of God to bring new life. Trustworthy preaching is faithful and effective. As discussed in the preface, faithful preaching ensures that the gospel is proclaimed and heard. During congregational transitions, preaching is effective when it serves as a powerful tool for leading the congregation's journey through the transition and points to a faithful response to both the challenges and the opportunities the transition brings.

That faithful preaching can be an effective tool in leading congregational transitions may seem obvious. Theologically, the preaching of God's Word constitutes the congregation as a faith community. Preaching is a primary way that God forms the congregation and the congregation witnesses to its faith. We find testimony to the centrality of preaching in the life of the Christian community as early as the description of the Pentecost church in Acts: "[T]hose who welcomed [Peter's] message were baptized, and that day about three thousand persons were added. They devoted themselves to the apostles' teaching and fellowship, to the breaking of bread and the prayers" (Acts 2:41-42). Ideally, both pastor and congregation regularly experience preaching as a community-forming event because preaching provides a path of discernment, rather than a hermetically sealed conclusion delivered from on high. In practical terms, preaching is the chief responsibility of the pastor and the principal way that the pastor and congregation *together* reflect upon their faith and common life.

The centrality of preaching to the life of the church leads Mark Olson, a Lutheran pastor, to suggest that mainline Christians seeking to claim an identity in an ever-changing world might find that radical identity by being deeply rooted in their faith tradition.[1] Olson reminds us that we are called to preach the gospel of Jesus that offers unconditional hope and to administer the sacraments, which are a visible word of grace. We are called to teach Bible stories about a God who continually transforms the world, and to trust God to work through the simple acts of preaching, worshiping, teaching, and praying. Claiming the radical identity that is deeply rooted in the congregation's faith tradition is particularly important during congregational transitions. Preaching is essential to this radical identity. Trusting the partnership of preaching and congregational transition will benefit the congregation in numerous ways; however, this trust also involves certain risks.

Benefits of Preaching in Congregational Transition

The use of preaching to lead a congregation through transition is beneficial to the congregation in several ways. *First,* in the midst of transition, the preaching event can be an occasion when the congregation experiences God's presence, grace, power, and direction. Through preaching, the congregation can move from attempting to explain the transition to exploring the transition to experience God in it. If we think of the transition as a haunted house, then preaching, rather than explaining why we should not be afraid of the house, allows us to go inside, to open the doors, to see what is there, and to bring it into the realm of God. Preaching can help the congregation illuminate the mystery inherent in the transition, rather than seeking to eliminate it, so that God provides orientation and direction as the congregation moves into what is still unknown.

Second, building on Bridges's model of transition, preaching potentially affords a corresponding benefit for each strand of the transition. As change brings on a transition, preaching can serve as a means of disclosing, of providing information, and of giving assurance by anchoring the change in God's faithfulness and the congregation's life of faith. Recall that when a change occurs, the congregation will ideally move from ending its old identity and practices through a liminal strand to a new beginning. In the ending strand, preaching is a powerful way to enable the congregation to express lament. In the liminal strand, preaching can help to name the ambiguities of the transition and celebrate the truth of God's ongoing presence and purpose. As the congregation moves into a new beginning, preaching is a dynamic means of imaging a picture of the congregation's new vision and reality. Like the transitional strands themselves, these benefits are less sharply defined than the way I present them here. Providing information, expressing lament, celebrating God's faithfulness amid named ambiguities, and offering a vision of the new reality are ongoing, overlapping benefits of preaching in congregational transition. Each of these benefits becomes more or less prominent, depending on the congregation and its location on the journey of transition.

Third, preaching invites the congregation to respond to God's grace by participating in a process of discovery and decision. Inviting the congregation to respond in faith is distinct from proclaiming what has already been decided and pontificating on what the congregation needs to do. Rather than stifling conversation and polarizing the assembly on various sides of an agenda, preaching in times of transition casts a vision, grounds the transition theologically, and orients and mobilizes the community of faith. As part of this process, preaching gives voice to the congregation, naming its ambivalent feelings, fears, hopes, questions, doubts, and expressions of faith. This voice in preaching signals to the members of the congregation that God understands everything they are experiencing and that their feelings are valued in the process of transition.

Fourth, as an act of nonviolent resistance to the powers of death and destruction, preaching is one way the congregation resists those forces that seek to silence and divide it, and to undermine, sidetrack, and derail its transition. Charles Campbell observes that, from the very beginning, the Word of God is set over against violent domination. As God begins the first creation through the Word, God inaugurates the new creation through Jesus Christ, the Word made flesh. Jesus, as the incarnation of the Word, embodies God's way not merely in his life but most specifically in his choice of

preaching as the means to the reign of God.[2] Both the form and content of
Jesus' preaching declare that God's way is neither silent passivity and acceptance nor coerced belief, forced agenda, and dominating control. Jesus' life
and preaching allow humans the freedom of decision, choice, and expression. By using preaching to proclaim God's reign, Jesus requires and demonstrates mutuality, the participation of the one speaking and the ones
listening. Jesus' preaching refuses to treat the listener as an object or com-
modity. Jesus' preaching does not coerce or control its outcome. Jesus nonetheless chooses to work through preaching, rather than through absolute
constraints, to inaugurate God's new beginning. Like the preaching of Jesus,
the church's preaching of Christ is itself a way congregations resist attempts
to control the journey of transition and attempts to force an outcome and
a way they resist all those forces trying to divide, dishearten, and disas-
semble the community of faith.

Finally, preaching centered in the gospel calls both congregation and
pastor to focus on God rather than on results. Faithfulness and the results
we hope for and value do not necessarily go hand in hand. As Mark Olson
observes, "It is true that, when Peter preaches at Pentecost, three thousand
are baptized. Yet, it is also true that, when Stephen preaches, he is stoned to
death."[3] Achieving measurable results is certainly an essential part of managing transitions. Sadly, when pastors and congregations do not see the
results they hope for or anticipate, they may feel inadequate and unfaithful.
Preaching grounded in the gospel assures both pastor and congregation
that achieving measurable results is not the ultimate goal of either preaching or congregational transition. Through preaching, the need and desire
for measurable results are balanced by the gospel's assurance; we are not
made right with God by our results. The gospel's assurance calls us to what
is often a harder task. When we believe that our congregation has a particular, God-given vocation, and we are striving to be faithful to that vocation,
the gospel calls us to trust God even when we feel quite discouraged, "not
[to] grow weary in doing what is right" (Gal. 6:9), and to remain alert to the
ways that God shares and sustains us in our calling. For the gospel calls us
to be open to God's Spirit, to say and do what we know to be true, to live in
a way that is congruent with the gospel, and to be faithful to the life of
Christ, regardless of the results.

Faithful and effective preaching assures the congregation of God's presence and participation and provides a powerful impetus to carrying out

the tasks of each strand of the transition. By centering the congregation's life in God and not in results, preaching also invites the congregation to respond to God's grace through participation in the transition as an unfolding journey, and equips the congregation to resist those forces that seek to destroy it. In these ways, preaching enfolds the congregational transition into God's never-ending work of transformation. Thus, preaching is a beneficial means of leading congregational transitions.

Risks of Preaching in Congregational Transition

While preaching in times of congregational transition may lead to transformation, preaching is risky because of the ways in which it can potentially paralyze and polarize the congregation.

First, preaching about the transition may escalate the sense of crisis. Stated simply, preaching may cause the congregation both a crisis of understanding and a crisis of decision. When preaching questions, challenges, or contradicts the congregation's understanding of God's will and God's nature, or when preaching does not address the transition, possibly leaving the impression that God has nothing to say, the congregation may experience a crisis of understanding. When preaching does not give the congregation time to formulate its response to transition, or help the congregation to do so, or when preaching offers only a single way of responding, which some members may find difficult or disagree with, a crisis of decision may result.

Second, preaching about the transition may create factions or even split the congregation. Rather than entering into the transitional process as an unfolding journey, people may take sides according to whether they agree with the sermon, support the pastor, feel comforted or convicted by the preaching, or consider it appropriate for the pastor to address the transition from the pulpit. This outcome is especially likely if the congregation would rather avoid or deny the changes it needs to face.

Third, controversy and division may render the church and its worship "unsafe." Preaching and the transition may undermine the hospitality, forgiveness, understanding, acceptance, and unity that Christian worship intends to embody. Rather than being a refuge from the changes and chances of life and a reflection of God's reign, the church and its worship may become an arena for combat or the battleground in a civil war.

Most important, addressing the transition in preaching too much, too often, or too aggressively may replace or drown out the gospel. When the sermon's spotlight shines so brightly on the congregation or the transition that God is left in the dark, when the emphasis is on what the congregation needs to do rather than on what God has done and is doing, the gospel may be inaudible to the congregation. On the other hand, ignoring the transition or addressing it too minimally may render the pulpit and the gospel irrelevant to the situation and to real life. Finding this balance is one of the greatest challenges of preaching in times of congregational transition.

Minimizing these risks is a principal reason that preachers engage in "holy and active listening" before they ever utter a word from the pulpit (see chapter 4). Even when preaching is flawless, the health of the congregation and the dynamics of the change and transition may make it impossible to avoid these risks totally. At the same time, preachers minimize these risks by demanding of themselves that the gospel be the core of their preaching. To preach the gospel with power, authenticity, and relevance, preachers vigilantly attend to the congregation, the change and transition, and their own inner world. Nurturing this attentiveness, which in chapter 4 I call "holy and active listening," is essential to vigilance and proportion.

Faced with the benefits and risks of using preaching to address the transition, and recognizing that the transition will find its way into preaching, preachers must decide when and how to address the transition from the pulpit. They need to determine the appropriate time. They must also negotiate the difficult middle ground between ignoring the transition in their preaching on the one hand and obsessing about the transition on the other. Ultimately, these are the preacher's decisions. At the same time, these decisions are best made in consultation with other leaders responsible for guiding the congregation through transition, particularly the congregational council or board.

DEFINING THE PARTNERSHIP

Confronted by a transition, a congregation often has only two choices: walk forward in boldness or cower in fear. The gospel calls and empowers the congregation to go forward boldly in faith. The question, of course, is how to forge a relationship between preaching and the transition that can be trusted to empower the congregation to move ahead in faith. Over the course of the transition, various approaches will be necessary. At times preachers will address the transition with forethought and intention. Spontaneity and improvisation will also be necessary, as when the transition surfaces unexpectedly in the preaching and when the preacher must respond quickly to the unanticipated. In some sermons the transition will be set aside.

David Schlafer, an Episcopal priest and teacher of preaching, provides four strategies for addressing occasions in preaching. These are equally applicable to defining the possible relationships of preaching and transition—preaching *around*, preaching *about*, preaching *at*, and preaching *through*.[4]

Preaching *around* can be both harmful and necessary. When we preach *around*, we ignore the change and transition, treating the unavoidable as though it were simply not there. Or we deal with issues at the periphery of the transition, rather than at its heart. Stated more positively, we decide that it is best not to address the transition in a particular sermon or only to acknowledge it in a cursory way so that the preaching remains gospel-centered and does not become agenda-driven. This approach will not work as a long-term strategy, however, because the voice of the transition will not remain silent. On the contrary, it will press harder and harder to be heard. If the transition is never addressed in preaching, a congregation may conclude that God has nothing to say at critical times in its life; congregants may lose interest in what God has to say at other times. At the same time, in the course of a congregational transition, the transition will not be the focus of every sermon; sometimes it may not even be mentioned explicitly. On occasion, ignoring a transition in a sermon is the most effective way of helping the process, as when the congregation needs a respite from the work of transition or has agreed simply to listen for God's guidance for a time.

Preaching *about* is preaching that makes the transition the primary, if not exclusive, subject of every sermon. Preachers become so obsessed with the change and transition that explaining the transition and telling the congregation how to respond to it becomes the sermon's purpose. For example, one pastor chose to devote a sermon to an architectural presentation of the proposed building expansion. When the function of the sermon is to preach *about* the transition, the hearing of the gospel is diminished, if not lost. This obsession can also distract the congregation's energy and attention from the very things the preacher intends to address. Often, this kind of preaching provides a single, seemingly airtight theological framework for understanding the issue or transition, and lays out *the* appropriate way to respond. Since preaching about the transition is so information-laden, it tends to diminish the congregation's experience of God's presence in this time and place. While congregations certainly need to give and receive information about the transition, this need is best met in venues other than the pulpit.

Preaching *at* the transition occurs when the preacher makes the congregation's presumed concerns and feelings about the transition the content of the sermon. For example, in response to a tragedy in the community, a pastor delivers an overview of the stages of grief as the sermon. This approach confuses preaching with counseling that provides either comfort or correction. While comfort and correction may be the effects of a sermon, they result from the proclamation of the gospel. They are ways we experience God's presence and purpose; they are not the explicit content of the sermon. Preaching at the transition often causes members of the congregation to feel awkward and self-conscious as their private feelings and responses are named in so public a way. As a result, the congregation does not hear what the preacher is saying.

Finally, preaching *through* the transition is sensitive to the history behind the transition, and to the possible futures it opens up. This does not mean that the sermon retells the story of transition from beginning to end. Nor does the sermon issue a detailed roadmap of the future. Rather, preaching through transition is mindful of the movement and flow of the transition as an open-ended journey. Preaching *through* the transition approaches the transition as a "window" that provides a fresh perspective on the grace of God, and the grace of God as a "window" that provides a new vision of, and orientation in, the transition.

With David Schlafer, we commend preaching *through* as the best way of addressing a congregational transition from the pulpit because this approach best guarantees that God remains the essential proclamation. One danger of recommending a single model of preaching is that people immediately look for and find preachers and sermons that use the opposite approach quite effectively. Although preaching *around,* preaching *at,* and preaching *about* may serve as tools for preaching *through* a congregational transition, and although one can find examples of sermons in which these strategies worked effectively by themselves, if preachers do not set out to preach the gospel, the chances are good that they will preach something else.

Preaching *through* a congregational transition is the most consistent way of preaching the gospel. In the next two chapters, we will examine how one preaches through a transition. Before turning to sermon preparation, we will explore a final aspect of the partnership between preaching and congregational transition; namely, the ways preaching cooperates with other processes used to lead the transition.

PREACHING AS PART OF A LARGER PROCESS

Given people's ability to forget and deny difficult realities, we cannot trust a single experience either to bring permanent change or to sustain a change that has begun.[5] Leading a congregation through transition requires patience, repetition, and sustained effort. Throughout the transition, the congregation needs to be reminded of God's presence in the transition, the changes the transition brings, the promise of resurrection, and the new identity and mission that may result.

Preaching through a transition is itself a process. A single sermon will not suffice. Rather, the transition must be an integral and ongoing part of the congregation's preaching ministry. That a single sermon is never sufficient to move a congregation through transition becomes obvious when we consider the nature of preaching. Christians need to be reminded of the gospel; they need to hear again and again the difference that Christ's life, death, and resurrection make for their lives and for the life of the world. For this reason, we preach at least once a week rather than once in people's lifetimes. No matter how powerful a sermon is, its power fades; its impact diminishes. The congregation will need another sermon. More important, preaching alone is not enough to move a congregation through a time of transition. At one time, advertisers told us that people need to receive a message eight times in three different ways for the message to stick. More recent reports indicate that these numbers have increased dramatically as we have been bombarded with more and more information—and have become more adept at tuning it out. Preaching must therefore be part of a larger ministry. Like the body of Christ itself, this ministry is made up of many parts (see Eph. 4:12-16).

Transition and the Many Parts of Ministry

Though preaching is central to a congregation's life, the full expression of Christian community encompasses numerous activities. Congregational life includes worship, Bible study, fellowship, one-on-one and small-group relationships, service, stewardship, outreach, and social justice. These groups and activities can all be enlisted to lead the congregation through a transition. For example, the congregation might use existing small groups to provide information, minimize isolation, foster communication, and maintain connections between members and leaders. When using existing groups and activities to manage a transition, leaders must be careful not to prefer or appear to prefer one group to another so that the members of the congregation feel that they are in the transition together.

Pastors know that, in the normal course of a congregation's life, preaching works in partnership with these activities so that the congregation is formed by and witnesses to the gospel. A stewardship campaign, for example, always involves at least one stewardship sermon. In times of congregational transition, leaders can employ the collaboration of preaching and the activities of congregational life to lead the congregation effectively through transition. For example, the preacher might raise issues in a sermon that are subsequently discussed in existing groups. This approach recognizes that preaching in particular and worship in general are ill-suited for the transmission of extensive information and as occasions for extended conversation and dialogue.

As a partner in congregational transition, preaching also collaborates with those processes consciously created as means of leading the transition. I outlined in chapter 1 the purposes of these processes. They include giving people opportunities to name their losses and providing leaders with ways to discover why people are resisting change (ending strand); helping people to negotiate chaos while simultaneously encouraging creativity (liminal strand); and providing a vision and inviting participation (new beginning). Leaders endeavor to fulfill these purposes by providing opportunities for the congregation to hear about and experience firsthand the new reality brought on by change, scheduling times when members of the congregation can voice their questions, concerns, and feelings; and creating events and actions that dramatize the endings, liminal strands, and new beginnings. One congregation celebrated its history by making a butcher-paper time line that covered the entire wall of its fellowship hall. The years of the congregation's life were marked on the time line, and people wrote significant events in their lives and in the life of the congregation at the appropriate place. People told stories, and the congregation cherished its past. Then a future time line was posted. The congregation wrote in hopes and dreams on this time line, then began determining priorities and considering strategies for attaining them.

Another congregation added a special column to its newsletter aimed at helping members understand their feelings about the transition. Those articles considered such topics as the signs and symptoms of grieving, the freedom and permission that accompany the confusion and fear caused by chaos, and the assurance that it is OK to feel sad when good things are happening. A third congregation created an image of its mission statement and used it on everything from banners to T-shirts to the congregation's letterhead.

Of particular importance is William Bridges's advice to institutions in transition to establish a team whose sole purpose is to monitor the transition.[6] This monitoring team is distinct from and in addition to the team managing the change. In fact, congregational leaders need to make clear to both the congregation and the monitoring team itself that this is not a decision-making group. Leadership must also ensure that the concerns voiced by the monitoring team do not disappear. The monitoring team should include the widest cross section of members possible. Establishing such a team shows the congregation that its leadership wants to know how things are going. The monitoring team also provides a focus group to review plans before they are announced, and it can be a channel to correct misinformation and to counter rumors.

Finally, pastoral care is itself an essential process for leading congregational transitions. When the minister is pastorally available, easily approachable, and open rather than defensive in responding to people's questions, feelings, and concerns, pastoral conversations provide a natural and important way for members of the congregation to give and receive information and to express feelings about the transition. In some congregations, the conversations that occur between pastor and congregant as part of teaching, visitation, committee work, and chance encounters in the community are the most important means of leading transitions. Of course, clergy and other leaders cannot use pastoral conversations to manipulate. At the same time, leaders need to recognize the important role that these conversations play in leading congregational transitions. Leaders should also recognize that, in addition to the pastor, church administrative assistants, parish administrators, and other staff members, as well as congregational elders, routinely serve this pastoral function for some people. Finally, pastors and other leaders must be careful to guard against both violating confidentiality and engaging in triangulation—"diverting conflict between two people by involving a third"[7]—particularly as these conversations inform preaching.

Preaching and Other Processes

Whether the processes used to lead the congregation through transition are the normal activities of congregational life, mechanisms especially established to address the transition, or the important conversations that occur as part of pastoral ministry, preaching collaborates with these processes in three ways. First, transition processes inform preaching as listening posts. Second, preaching anchors these processes in the gospel. Third, preaching is either amplified or undermined by other congregational processes used to manage the transition.

Preachers who have led congregations through significant transitions report that the processes used to manage the transition provide essential *listening posts* for preaching. Preaching needs to be informed and shaped by the other processes used to lead the congregation as it seeks to address the transition. Preachers should perhaps participate in these processes more by listening than by speaking. The most obvious example of a listening post for preaching is the team used to monitor the transition. As a partner with preaching, the monitoring team provides a safe and recognized forum for soliciting and receiving both important congregational input (information, perceptions, and feelings) that will shape sermon content, form, and delivery and feedback on how the congregation receives and responds to the preaching. Every group that participates in the congregation's transition is a potential listening post for preaching. In fact, some preachers so value this collaboration that they make the connection between preaching and other processes obvious and concrete. Considering Scripture through the lens of transition becomes their approach to weekly Bible study, the theme of the devotions they use to begin meetings, and a topic for conversation during pastoral visits. These preachers include feedback forms in worship folders, schedule Sunday morning forums to discuss their sermons with the congregation, and create threaded discussions on the Internet. Their purpose is clear; they want to become better preachers. In chapter 4, I will have much more to say about both the essential role that listening plays in preparing the transitional sermon and what the preacher should listen for.

At the same time that other processes are informing preaching, preaching *anchors* those other processes in the gospel. Preaching frames and empowers the processes used to lead the congregation through transition by grounding them in God's call and the congregation's response. In preaching the congregation hears that processes used to lead the transition are not ends in themselves. Rather, they are ways the congregation forms its life and carries out its mission. As such, congregational processes are expressions of God's ongoing work of making all things new. In this way, preaching holds other processes accountable to the gospel that is preached. If, for example, the preacher declares that God's unconditional love frees us to ask hard questions, express our concerns and feelings, and attempt new ventures without fear of ridicule from within the faith community, then the events and activities by which the congregation participates in the transition need to be safe gatherings in which these things can happen.

Processes used to lead the transition *amplify* or *undermine* preaching. When preaching and the congregation's other processes are congruent, the message of the sermon is amplified. The role preaching plays in leading the congregational transition is enhanced because the congregation experiences the pulpit as a place where the truth is spoken, and preaching as something that leadership takes seriously. On the other hand, when preaching and the congregation's other processes are not congruent, people trust their own experience more than the preacher's words. The role that preaching plays in the transition is diminished because the sermon's message is undermined or even contradicted by the practices of the faith community.

Understanding the processes used to lead a congregation through transition as preaching's listening post and amplifier, and preaching as the anchor that grounds these processes, is neither revolutionary nor original. This partnership characterizes all preaching. We highlight these three ways of understanding the relation of preaching and congregational life because, like all people, preachers need truths repeated if their message is to be reinforced.

Preaching and Worship

Of all the processes that might be used to lead a congregation through transition, none is more closely aligned with preaching than the congregation's worship. Most often, preaching occurs within a worship context. Today the church increasingly considers preaching to be integral to Christian worship, rather than being either the "main event" for which everything else in worship is but window dressing, or a self-contained entity that interrupts the flow of worship.[8] It is therefore appropriate to consider more fully the special relation of preaching and worship, especially in relation to a congregational transition.

Elsewhere I have written about this relationship in more detail.[9] To summarize, Christian worship is a corporate action through which the congregation gives praise and thanksgiving to God for salvation achieved and offered. This praise and thanksgiving centers on remembering God's intervention in human history, particularly through salvation in Jesus Christ. Recalling that gift of salvation, the congregation asks God to continue to remember us here and now, and offers praise, thanksgiving, and service to Christ in the world. As such, Christian worship both forms and reflects the congregation's faith. Mark Olson observes: "The way a congregation gathers, prays, hears God's Word proclaimed, sings, and shares in the Lord's Supper and Holy Baptism determines who they are and how they will live out their life together. Worship crafts the congregation's character by inviting the community of faith to surrender itself to God."[10]

Preaching and worship work together to form and reflect the congregation's faith in at least five ways.

First, worship prepares the congregation to hear the sermon. The call to worship, the music, and the prayers that precede the reading of Scripture and the sermon help to form the congregation from a gathering of individuals into the body of Christ. As the congregation worships together before the sermon, it is centered in and opened to God.

Second, preaching is dependent on the congregation's worship, just as it is dependent on the church's Scripture. Effective preaching is the servant of the church's Scriptures and enables the assembly to worship in a more meaningful and committed manner. The style of the congregation's worship imposes constraints on the form of preaching. For example, in most congregations, the sermon cannot be two hours long. A formal worship style may dictate a more formal style of preaching. At the same time, the familiarity and stability of the worship service afford preaching a certain freedom and boldness as the preacher seeks to bring home the Christian message imaginatively and penetratingly to a particular group of people at this time and in this place.

Third, the congregation's worship teaches the preacher how to make theological concepts such as praise, salvation, grace, sin, and repentance concrete and accessible when the preacher uses what the congregation does in worship as concrete models of these concepts. For example, confession and absolution in worship provide a concrete expression of forgiveness. We confess that we have sinned, rebelled against God, acted selfishly toward others, neglected the poor, and ignored creation. In the name of God we are declared forgiven and given another chance. In this way and so many others, worship envisions a reordering of the world according to God's intent. By putting a vision of the reign of God before God's people, worship also exposes injustices and contradictions between our faith and our way of living. These revelations are powerful and transforming because the congregation actively participates in them and is not merely told about them.

Fourth, the sermon and the other parts of Christian worship, including hymns, gestures, and environment, complement one another in the ways they proclaim the gospel. Whereas preaching speaks though the ears to the mind and heart, the objects, gestures, and outward signs of Christian worship reach the members of the congregation through their other senses. This is particularly evident in the ways children participate in worship, but all people are moved by the beauty of music and architecture. Singing unites the congregation and teaches the faith in ways the preached Word cannot. Regardless of its style, all Christian worship is multisensory.

Finally, worship is the first and perhaps the most appropriate activity for responding to the good news we hear in the sermon because the liturgy both shows us how to give God thanks and praise and gives us the opportunity to do so. We might think of Christian worship as our "dress rehearsal" for life in God's reign. Through preaching, we are taught how to put the Scriptures into effect in our daily lives. Hymns, prayers, creed, and sacraments provide our first opportunity to do so. For example, in the Western pattern of Holy Communion, our first opportunity to declare our intention to live the vision proclaimed in the sermon is the congregation's corporate intercessions. In its prayers, the congregation commits itself to work for those things that it asks of God—peace, justice, healing, and the spread of the gospel.

In all these ways, elements of the worship service—including Scripture, music, creed, prayers, peace, offering, sacraments, and the worship space—provide a context for, and reinforce the message of, the sermon and supply the congregation with the words, actions, and opportunity to respond to that message in faith. Although preachers should always take care to coordinate all the elements of worship to ensure that they support and reinforce each other, this coordination is especially important in times of congregational transition because of the ways the elements of the worship service can be enlisted to support both the preaching and the transition.

First, when we say things about God, faith, the change, and the transition in the worship service, we may not need to say them in the sermon. More important, sometimes we can say things about God, faith, the change, and the transition in the worship service that we cannot say in the sermon. At a point when we may not be ready or able to take a position in the sermon, we can acknowledge and bring that position before God in prayer. This is particularly true in times of war, when we pray for our enemies, for those who hate and want to hurt us. Prayers serve as an effective entry point for bringing dimensions of the transition into worship. Once issues are raised in prayer, they can more easily find their way into the sermon.

Worship can effectively strengthen and reinforce the sense of Christian community so necessary for moving a congregation through transition. Praying for those leading the transition and thanking God for the congregation's faithful response strengthen the sense that everyone is in this venture together. An extended sharing of the peace gives congregational members the opportunity to express their unity in Christ using word and touch. Favorite hymns unite the congregation in song and conjure memories of its common life beyond the present situation. Litanies give people the opportunity to speak what is on their heart. Finally, the worship space itself supports community when it is arranged so that people face those in whose lives they have a stake.

Prayer vigils and interfaith services are particularly important ways of addressing change and transition that cause a crisis of understanding. When it is unclear how the congregation should respond, when the congregation is divided over how it should respond, or when the faithful response runs counter to what is natural, obvious, and most practically beneficial, gathering to pray is essential to moving forward. Congregational, ecumenical, and interfaith services all provide important ways of witnessing to the greater community and beginning dialogue among people of faith who share different perspectives. Prayer gives people unwilling or unable to serve in any other way a significant means of participating in the transition. Silent prayer in worship is an especially powerful way of bringing people into God's presence, opening them to God's Spirit, and uniting the congregation in the One who transcends both the situation and responses to it.

Children's sermons are a natural way of including the congregation's children in the transition. Pastors can use children's sermons to address the transition and its connection to the faith simply, succinctly, and directly. In these moments, the pastor can lift up questions, fears, and concerns that only children will name but that everyone else is feeling. As always, adults will be overhearing and gleaning wisdom from the pastor's conversation with the kids.

The prayers said over the bread and wine of communion and the water of baptism speak to a God of change and highlight the transitional nature of God's people. Our God brought Noah and his family safely through the waters of the flood, and led Israel through the sea from slavery to freedom. Our God sent prophets to call for change and then Jesus, who changed death into life and despair into hope. As God's people remember and celebrate baptism and receive the bread and cup, we are changed ourselves and called to participate in God's ongoing work of changing the world. With God we strive to bring life out of death, speech out of silence, hope out of despair, and light out of darkness as we participate in the greatest transition, God's changing the world from the world as it is to the world as God intends it to be.

Finally, Scripture is foundational to the life and worship of the people of God. I discussed in chapter 1 the value of speaking of the change and transition using biblical stories and images. In chapter 3, I explore how the preacher selects and studies Scripture for preaching during a congregational transition. Here I commend the creative and thoughtful use of Scripture in worship. Regardless of whether congregations use the lectionary for preaching, the imaginative and sound use of Scripture in prayers, litanies, call to worship, call to confession, assurance of forgiveness, and benediction can accomplish much in moving the congregation through transition. Employing Scripture in these ways can powerfully reinforce the message of the sermon and liturgy, address the transition without mentioning it explicitly in the sermon, and provide worshipers with the words to express their feelings, questions, doubts, and praise.

Though by no means exhaustive, these possibilities illustrate the important role that worship plays as a congregation moves through transition. As we consider worship as the context of preaching in times of congregational transition, however, perhaps we feel the return of the anxiety that we attempted to set aside at the start of this chapter. This Sunday's service and sermon need to be prepared. It is time to bring the transition into our process of sermon preparation.

Questions for Reflection

- Are there times in your ministry when preaching has felt more like exploring than explaining? How did exploring show itself in your sermons?
- Name an occasion when preaching felt risky. Why was preaching risky? What was the risk?
- Name three groups or activities that are important to the life of your congregation. Identify a way that each of these three could be enlisted to lead a transition.
- Identify three ways that preaching and worship support one another in your context. Name three ways that the interaction of preaching and worship could be improved.

CHAPTER 3

THE SERMON IN TRANSITION

Now *we* are the preachers staring at blank computer screens or empty legal pads as we sit down to write our sermons. We acknowledge that the congregational transition will be part of our preaching. We trust preaching enough to invite that transition to be an active participant in the preparation and delivery of the sermon. But how do we proceed? What method should we follow?

As I have said, at its best, preaching through congregational transition invites the listeners to respond to God's grace by discovering God in change and transition and deciding how to respond in faith. Preaching through transition does not downplay change or eliminate transition by declaring what has already been decided and what the congregation needs to do. Rather, preachers proclaim God's grace amid change and lead the congregation to respond to that grace by participating in the transition as an act of faith. The methods that preachers use for this purpose are as unique as the preachers themselves and their communities of faith. In this chapter, I attempt to help preachers discover their unique ways of preaching through congregational transition by offering a combination of new ideas and preaching fundamentals. This approach reflects the coupling of stability and creativity that characterizes the process of preparing the transitional sermon. The first step is for preachers to consider their own method of sermon preparation.

KNOW YOUR METHOD

A method of sermon preparation is an orderly process that leads preachers from their initial reflections on Scripture in light of the community of faith and the world through discerning and crafting the message to delivering the sermon.[1] One way or another, all methods of sermon preparation include selecting and studying Scripture, determining the central message, creating the manuscript, and delivering the sermon. Regardless of whether preachers can articulate their method of sermon preparation or analyze what it is, Barbara Brown Taylor, Episcopal priest and adjunct professor at Columbia Theological Seminary, accurately observes that "every preacher has a different routine for preparing the sermon."[2] Confronted by a congregational transition, we do not necessarily have before us the task of learning a new method of sermon preparation and delivery. One pastor recalled:

> When the transition hit, I was in major panic mode. I told myself that things were so difficult in the congregation and in our lives that I needed to tap into the newest trends in homiletics to get through this. Then a wise parishioner reminded me that I know how to preach and told me not to panic. She said that the last thing the congregation needed was for me to veer from my normal style. It was like she was waving a road sign that told me to stay on course and not detour.

Rather than learn a new approach to preaching, we need to decide how the transition will be incorporated into and influence our regular routine of preparing the sermon. It is essential that preachers be honest with themselves and identify their actual routine, rather than calling up the method they wish they could follow or have been told they ought to use. For example, translating the entire passage of Scripture on which the sermon is based from Hebrew or Greek may not be part of every preacher's weekly preparation. Many preachers never write a manuscript. I know that the four hours I spend every Saturday evening memorizing my manuscript is not an aspect of sermon preparation that every preacher feels compelled to embrace.

One way that preachers can uncover their actual method of sermon preparation is to recall or—even better when time permits—record what they do to prepare their sermons each day during the week before they preach. If the preaching event takes place on Sunday morning, the week begins on the previous Sunday afternoon, preferably with rest. From this daily log, preachers can reconstruct their actual method of sermon preparation. Many find that periodically reviewing their routine in this way keeps their preaching fresh, as well as ensuring that it is a priority of their ministry.

Once they can articulate their way of preparing the sermon, preachers are free to examine and reevaluate their method. They might ask, How is my method of sermon preparation and delivery working? What about it do I affirm? What about it might I like to rethink or change? What am I neglecting? What would I like to try? Daring preachers might share their methods with the people they serve and ask their listeners to reflect on what is working and where there is room for growth.

Most important, perhaps, preachers should consider whether they trust God to work through their routine of sermon preparation and delivery. While preachers may wait for God to speak to them by shouting from the sky, most often God speaks to preachers through their method of preparing. A method of preaching enables us to seek divine inspiration by working as though preaching depends on us and by trusting God more than everything else, because ultimately preaching depends upon God. An essential but frequently overlooked part of any method, then, is giving the Holy Spirit opportunity to participate in the process. We invite the Holy Spirit into the process by allowing enough time to wait for God to speak to us. Often, we are the most attuned to God when we put ourselves in the places where the Spirit speaks to us and attend to the ways that insights bubble up. Experience—both my own and that of many preachers I have encountered—tells me that sermons rarely come to us as we fumble with keyboards or scribble on legal pads under deadline pressure. This observation seems particularly true when preaching through a congregational transition. In days of transition, when as preachers we feel frantic, we need to slow down just a bit and give ourselves the gift of listening for God to speak to us.

With our authentic method of sermon preparation before us, we are ready to explore how a congregational transition affects the creation and delivery of the sermon. First, I identify three paradoxes of preparing the transitional sermon. I then consider how a congregational transition affects selecting and studying Scripture, determining what to say, crafting the manuscript, and delivering the sermon.

PARADOXES OF PREPARING TRANSITIONAL SERMONS

A congregational transition affects a preacher's weekly routine in paradoxical ways. Preachers experienced with preaching through transitions have identified three characteristics of preparing the transitional sermon that, while contradictory, are nonetheless true. First, during congregational transitions, they preach at their best, while risking what makes them their best in order to become completely new preachers. Second, regardless of how they decide to preach, they trust God rather than themselves. Third, preachers need more time for sermon preparation when less time is available.

Preach at Our Best

First, preaching through a congregational transition requires preachers to be authentic, to be their best, and to become someone new. When preachers are at their best, their preaching inspires the congregation's trust and confidence in the pastor's leadership. Above all else, their preaching voice comes from within, from the core of their being. As one pastor declared, "For good or for ill, I can only be myself." The preaching voice includes more than vocal quality. It encompasses the form, content, and tone of our preaching; our physical presence; and our relationship with God, with ourselves, and with our listeners. Every preacher has many preaching voices. For example, most have a pastoral voice and a prophetic voice, an assuring voice and a challenging voice, a playful voice and a serious voice. By tapping into and drawing from their truest selves, preachers are able to speak in these and other voices. Grounded themselves, preachers are better attuned to the circumstances—in the congregation, the preacher, and the transition—that necessitate using a different voice. They can then more quickly identify which voice to use.

When preachers are at their best, they preach from their strengths. They know their gifts and abilities and use them well. They give the preaching task the time and energy it deserves, even when the transition is pulling them in many directions. Preachers at their best do not start from scratch or experiment for experimentation's sake. They employ everything at their disposal that has proved to be faithful and effective. The discussion of preaching and its partners in chapter 2 reminds us that we have at our disposal strengths and abilities unrelated to preaching itself. For example, we may have a strong pastoral relationship with the congregation, an ability to see all sides, and a way of empowering others. To be our best in the pulpit, we draw upon all of our gifts.

At the same time, preachers stand ready to modify their approach to preaching when necessary. In fact, if they consider it the best course of action, preachers give themselves permission to abandon their method and become different preachers. After hearing the congregation's request for an interpretation of the change and transition that they could grapple with, a preacher who had prided himself on preaching that builds a consensus and supports others' exercise of their gifts and callings decided to abandon his own gifts. Instead, this preacher clearly named both his understanding of the transition and the process the congregation would follow in deciding how to respond to it. Though this approach was personally difficult for the preacher, it was what the congregation needed to move ahead. In choosing to modify or abandon their established patterns, preachers are mindful of the place of innovation in preaching. While a noticeable difference in technique can itself be striking, the creativity, boldness, and risk that a new approach to preaching requires are tools for preaching through transition; they are not ends in themselves.

On those occasions when the nature of the transition, the preacher's own place in the process, or the message that needs to be delivered prevents preachers from being their authentic best or becoming what is needed, they embrace the possibility that inviting a guest preacher is the appropriate way to preach through the transition. This approach may be called for when the pastor is the cause of the change and transition, or when the preacher is so personally caught up in the change that it becomes difficult or impossible to preach. A guest preacher also empowers the pastor to lead and set an example by joining the congregation in listening as another proclaims and invites the congregation to respond to God's presence and grace in the transition.

Trust God above All Else

Second, even as preachers strive to be their authentic best, ultimately they trust neither themselves nor any method or plan. Instead, they trust the power of the Word of God proclaimed. As one pastor declared, "Preaching in times of transition is so fraught with possibilities and peril that, in my experience as preacher, I am drawn to my reliance upon God, in whom I put my faith." Such reliance is particularly important when one feels unsure or lacks confidence. In those moments, preachers trust God to be faithful and to equip them and the congregation with what is needed. They trust that God is at work, regardless of their ability to preach well or the congregation's ability to listen well on a particular day. They trust that what is "coming in" to the preacher is what is supposed to "go out" in the sermon. They preach what their head knows until their heart believes. The paradox is that, as much as we trust the power of preaching and our best selves as preachers, we approach preaching with great humility. We are aware of limitations and mortality—the transition's, our own, and the sermon's. We arduously seek to remain centered in and dependent on God. In chapter 5, I will have more to say about remaining anchored in God amid the chaos of congregational transition.

Use Time Wisely

Our third paradox involves the timing of sermon preparation. We have discussed the benefits and risks of preaching in times of congregational transition. These high stakes call for careful sermon preparation. At the same time, the fast pace of a congregational transition frequently makes finding time for sermon preparation difficult. There is less open time for reflection. The entire process of sermon preparation is characterized by an increased urgency and particular attention to emotional coloring. It is not enough for preachers to determine what to say; even more important, they must seriously consider both the emotional connotation of the words they will use and the emotional climate in which the message will be received. On the one hand, the urgency and intensity lead some preachers to begin the process or to start writing earlier, even weeks in advance of the preaching event. On the other hand, they should not complete their preparation too early because the contours of the transition change in the course of hours and days, let alone a week.

Many preachers report that the pace of transition does not allow them to work on their sermons each day. They report that transitional sermons are often born in a single piece, a continuous flow. Rather than setting times to work on the sermon, these preachers spend much of the week editing in the head. Furthermore, since these sermons are not built on scriptural texts or written from church doctrine, traditional study is less important. Rather, these sermons grow out of the sum total of the transition and are sustained by life in God.

Both the uniqueness of each preacher and congregation and the paradoxes brought on by change and transition preclude our prescribing a single method of preaching through transition. We can, however, identify the ways a congregational transition affects the essential parts of every method of sermon preparation—selecting and studying Scripture, determining what to say, creating the manuscript, and delivering the sermon.

SELECT AND STUDY SCRIPTURE

During a congregational transition, deciding the purpose of the sermon and considering how the congregation will receive and respond to the sermon become more important than exegeting a passage of Scripture. The congregation, the change, and the transition provide the primary lenses through which Scripture is considered. At the same time, Scripture frames the change and transition, offering fresh insight, perspective, and direction. David Buttrick, professor emeritus of homiletics at Vanderbilt Divinity School, calls this kind of sermon "preaching the praxis mode." The preacher begins with a human situation rather than a text. Sermon preparation centers on "relating experience to gospel rather than gospel to experience." According to Buttrick, this kind of preaching "addresses persons *in* lived experience and, therefore, starts with a hermeneutic of lived experience."[3]

The notion that Scripture and the transition interpret one another assumes that, while the "original" or "historical" meaning of Scripture certainly contributes to preaching, it is not determinative because the Bible is more than an ancient document. In the words of Walter Brueggemann, we can approach the Bible as "a set of models (paradigms) of reality composed of images situated in and contextualized by narratives."[4] The purpose of these images is to lead the congregation into an alternative sense of God, world, neighbor, and self. Just as doctrines, theological traditions, liturgical seasons, and even the gospel itself shape how we approach Scripture, so too a congregational transition provides an appropriate lens through which to examine the Bible. The perils to be avoided in using this lens of interpretation are employing Scripture in ways contrary to the biblical witness and tradition and isolating Scripture or knitting passages together to "prove" a preferred agenda or a predetermined course of action.

Though the congregation, the change, and the transition are primary to preaching through a congregational transition, Scripture is nonetheless indispensable. David Bartlett, professor of preaching at Yale University Divinity School, unabashedly declares that "right preaching is the interpretation of Scripture." According to Bartlett, while excellent Christian speech might entertain, inform, inspire, and offer opinions in ways that help the faithful and edify the community, "unless [the sermon] is an interpretation of the text or texts that the congregation has just heard read aloud, it is not preaching."[5] I discussed in chapter 1 the powerful way that describing the congregation's transition using scriptural stories and images connects the transition to God's ongoing work of salvation. I said that the ample choices of biblical stories and images that address a particular transition provide many ways of approaching both Scripture and the transition. I observed that Scripture and the transition interpret each other, and encouraged preachers and congregations to expand the biblical texts they use to reflect upon the transition to gain greater perspective. Regardless of how Scripture is selected and studied, the biblical witness is an essential part of preaching through congregational transition.

Select the Text

I have asserted both that the congregation and transition are primary ingredients in the transitional sermon and that Scripture is indispensable to it. Many preachers respond that, while these are complementary assertions in theory, they are contradictory in practice. Their assumption is that preachers need to choose either Scripture or the transition as a starting point. Alternatively, the transition remains primary and Scripture essential when the particular text on which the sermon is based becomes negotiable. Selecting that text is the first decision the preacher must make. Stated simply, the preacher must decide whether the sermon will be lectionary-based, text-based, or topical.

A lectionary provides four appointed readings or lections (Old Testament, Psalm, Epistle, and Gospel) for every Sunday and festival of the Christian year. In the Revised Common Lectionary and its variations, these readings are arranged in a three-year cycle; over a three-year period, the faith community hears the Scripture texts that affirm the central themes of the Christian faith read in its worship. Some preachers develop their own "lectionaries," selecting the texts on which their sermons are based weeks and even months in advance. For many preachers attempting to find their footing amid the tremors of transition, the lectionary offers a solid place to stand. The lectionary provides order in the chaos of transition. It reminds both preacher and congregation that God's story and purpose are bigger than the circumstances they are facing. The lectionary also assists preachers and congregations to expand their biblical perspectives on the transition as they hear a greater breadth of Scripture over time. At the same time, the congregation's transition brings a fresh perspective and new life to the lectionary. In this way, preaching and the lectionary sustain each other. Sometimes preaching enlivens the lectionary; sometimes the lectionary enlivens preaching.

On those occasions when the appointed lections, whether for a given week or for a series of Sundays, do not address the congregation in transition, or when the connection between the lections and the transition is artificial at best, preachers may choose to set the appointed texts aside and select other passages of Scripture on which to base the sermon. In selecting texts for the transitional sermon, preachers should begin with their established method. For example, those that normally preach from the Revised Common Lectionary should seriously grapple with those texts before setting them aside. Similarly, preachers in the middle of a sermon series ought to explore ways of connecting the series and the transition before opting to cut the series short. When considering alternative Scripture texts to be read in worship, preachers need to be clear with themselves that the purpose of the sermon is to proclaim the gospel and to call the congregation to respond in faith to the challenges and opportunities of the transition. This clarity helps safeguard against both employing Scripture in ways contrary to the biblical witness and proof-texting to preach a single perspective or agenda. The selection of texts should exhibit respect for both the literary and theological unity of the Bible and the memories that have shaped the church's use of these particular passages. The preacher must decide how many texts will be read in worship, the purpose these readings are intended to serve, how the readings will relate to one another and what that relationship will signify, and how the occasion will give a context to these readings. Once the selections are made, the preacher needs boldly to claim the responsibility of the office of preacher for selecting the Scripture to be heard in worship. Timidity about a text's selection will only undermine its impact.

Finally, there are occasions and circumstances when topical preaching provides a helpful way to preach through a transition. "The topical sermon interprets a topic in light of the gospel but without originating or centering in the exposition of a biblical text or theme."[6] At its best, the topical sermon teaches the congregation how to interpret life in light of the gospel. It

models for the congregation how to name or identify an issue, reflect upon
it theologically, and claim changes in perception and behavior as a result of
that analysis. According to Ronald Allen, a topic "is a need, an issue, or a
situation which is important to the congregation (whether or not the congregation consciously recognizes its importance), which calls for interpretation from the perspective of the gospel, and which can better be addressed
from the standpoint of the gospel itself than from the standpoint of the
exposition of a particular passage (or passages) from the Bible."[7] Congregational transitions always meet two of Allen's criteria: they are important
to the congregation, and they need to be addressed from the perspective of
the gospel. The question that preachers need to consider is whether the best
way to address the transition is by using particular passages of Scripture or
by using a topical approach. In making this determination, preachers might
consider how much time they have to prepare and how urgently the congregation needs to understand and respond to the change and transition.
For example, when the community gathers to worship two days after its
church building burned to the ground, the congregation may need to hear
the gospel brought to bear on its situation more than it needs to hear an
exposition of a biblical text. In addition to weighing the congregation and
the situation, preachers should also consider whether Scripture speaks to
or is silent about an issue, whether the connection between Scripture and
sermon is tenuous, and whether the Bible will cause confusion or even harm.
The sermon preached on the Sunday after the congregation learned that its
matriarch had committed suicide might be such an occasion when a passage traditionally associated with suicide (Matt. 12:31-32) might do more
harm than good. Most important, rather than a random or expedient choice,
the decision to undertake a topical approach to preaching through a transition is "self-conscious, disciplined, [and] theologically mature."[8] Even when
preachers employ a topical approach, the transitional sermon should nonetheless be characterized by biblical allusions and references that place the
congregation's transition in the context of God's work of bringing creation
from death to new life.

Study Scripture

Just as we assume that preachers have an established method of sermon
preparation, so we also assume that preachers have a sound approach to

studying and interpreting Scripture. Congregational transitions are not occasions for abandoning these practices. On the contrary, like Scripture itself, established patterns of study offer an essential check against preaching what might be expedient, popular, burning in the preacher's heart, the correct answer, or best course of action, but not necessarily a word from God. At the same time, studying Scripture through the lens of congregational transition yields important insights into interpretation.

First, when we study and interpret Scripture using the lens of congregational transition, we see that ours is a transitional God and that we are called to be a people in transition. Considering Scripture from this perspective, we can expect established and inherited interpretation to be in tension with our experience. As I said earlier, Thomas Troeger grounds this tension in God because God will not be confined either to the Bible or to the past.[9] Scripture itself reveals that our God is faithfully committed to doing new things and acting in new ways to love, save, and renew God's people. God declares through the prophet Isaiah, "See, the former things have come to pass, and new things I now declare; before they spring forth, I tell you of them" (Isa. 42:9; see 43:19, 48:6). Through Ezekiel God promises, "A new heart I will give you, and a new spirit I will put within you" (Ezek. 36:26; see 11:19). Both Jeremiah and Jesus speak of a new covenant. Jeremiah declares, "The days are surely coming, says the Lord, when I will make a new covenant with the house of Israel and the house of Judah" (Jer. 31:31). Taking the cup after supper, Jesus speaks of "the new covenant in my blood" (Luke 22:20; cf. 1 Cor. 11:25). Jesus gives his disciples "a new commandment, that you love one another" (John 13:34). Paul declares, "So if anyone is in Christ, there is a new creation: everything old has passed away" (2 Cor. 5:17). The author of 1 Peter praises God who in "great mercy has given us a new birth into a living hope through the resurrection of Jesus Christ from the dead" (1:3). Both Isaiah and Revelation promise that God is "about to create new heavens and a new earth; the former things shall not be remembered or come to mind." (Isa. 65:17; see Rev. 21:1-2). Seated on the throne in the New Jerusalem, Jesus declares, "See, I am making all things new" (Rev. 21:5). Scripture reveals that our God faithfully acts in new ways and does new things. Thomas Troeger's claim, which bears repeating, is less jarring in this context. Troeger writes, "We have a technical term for people who do not change: dead. If Christ has not changed since the resurrection, then Christ is no longer alive."[10] Troeger calls preachers to cultivate the tension between inherited belief and contemporary experience as a way of opening themselves and their congregations to the living Christ.[11]

Second, in times of congregational transition, our approach to Scripture is more evocative than exegetical. We are more concerned with framing, reflecting on, and encountering God in the interplay of Scripture and the transition than in uncovering the original meaning of a text. Congregational transitions call preachers to encounter the Bible directly. While the original meaning of a text helps the preacher to understand Scripture, the more pressing question is how this passage of Scripture helps the congregation to understand and respond to the transition and how the congregation's experience of transition leads it to enter into the text. While the preacher's methods of exegesis are necessary, these alone are insufficient. Scripture must be active in the preacher's mind and heart as the preacher engages the congregation and transition. Sitting with and praying over the text, reading it over and over, and remaining alert to the ways the text speaks to and connects with what is happening in the transition is more useful than consulting the commentaries. Consciously reflecting on the text in light of the process used to lead the transition also brings new insight. For example, rather than constituting a defeat, could the congregation's decision not to follow a suggested course of action possibly be like the Spirit's telling Paul not to go on to Jerusalem? (Acts 21:4). In fact, the preacher might usefully read the text at congregational gatherings, during pastoral visits and conversations, at committee meetings, and in dialogue with the congregation's leadership and monitoring teams, and ask the people in these settings what the text says to them. Over time, the congregation might find that a particular Bible story has a familiar resonance, and claim it as the archetype of its transition. We are Abraham and Sarah, journeying to a land that the Lord will show us! (Gen. 12:1). We are like the disciples on Pentecost; filled with the Holy Spirit, we're ready to come out from behind locked doors (Acts 2). Like the woman at the well, this congregation is full of questions and uncertainties and pressing Jesus for answers (John 4).

As we saw in chapter 1, in some texts the transition is obvious—Israel's journey to the land of promise, Paul's trip to Damascus, Jonah's time in the belly of a fish. In other texts, the transition is subtle. The transition that went on in the life of a woman of Samaria as she talked with Jesus while drawing water (John 4) may become obvious only when we consider how this woman addresses Jesus. First, she calls Jesus "a Jew." Then she addresses him as "Sir." In the course of their conversation, this woman of Samaria refers to Jesus as "a prophet" and invites her neighbors to come and see if he might be "the Messiah." This woman seems to be moving from disdain toward belief. At other times the best way to uncover the transition is to imagine that what is happening in the text occurs within the context of the congregational transition. For example, in a congregation paralyzed by its commitment to long-established worship practices, the preacher retold the story of Jesus healing the bent-over woman in the synagogue on the Sabbath (Luke 13:10-17) as if it had happened during that congregation's worship. In the sermon, the preacher presented the leader of the synagogue as someone faithfully committed to the traditions and dignity of the community's worship.

This sympathetic portrayal of the leader of the synagogue reminds us that, once the transition is identified, the preacher should not be content with a single perspective. For example, if using Jesus' parable of the wicked tenants (Matt. 21:33-46; cf. Mark 12:1-12 and Luke 20:9-19), the preacher might invite the congregation to identify with both the tenants and the slaves. In this way, the preacher lifts up the various perspectives on the transition that the text provides. The preacher should be alert to the fact that Scripture may be silent on the particularities of the transition. One example: How should a congregation use an enormous bequest? Some passages of Scripture may even be harmful to a congregation in transition. We are talking here about those rare instances when the text of Scripture offers a perspective or course of action that is contrary to the gospel or morally inappropriate. For example, people often quote Deuteronomy 19:21 in response to an act of violence: "Show no pity: life for life, eye for eye, tooth for tooth, hand for hand, foot for foot." In instances like these, theologians Justo and Catherine González invite us to consider the direction of the action in the text and in the whole of Scripture. Rather than seeing a text as "a gem floating in a void," the Gonzálezes tell us to "place it in its historical setting, and ask the question of the direction of God's action in the text. Then, and only then, can we seek to apply the text to our own time."[12] In other words, we identify the transition in the text by discovering what God is ending and what God is beginning. To use Deuteronomy to guide our response to violence, we must recognize that God's intent in this law is to signal restraint. God's movement is from retaliation to a proportional response—*no more than* an eye for an eye and a tooth for a tooth. We also need to consider this passage in light of Jesus' words: "You have heard that it was said, 'An eye for an eye and a tooth for a tooth.' But I say to you, Do not resist an evildoer. But if anyone strikes you on the right cheek, turn the other also" (Matt. 5:38-39). Here Jesus moves from a proportional response to nonviolence. Understood in its proper context, this verse becomes less harmful to the congregation and may even become helpful. While the Gonzálezes encourage preachers to use this approach whenever they encounter potentially harmful texts, it is particularly helpful when preachers and congregations need to determine how a text does or does not specifically address a transition.

Third, congregational transitions invite preachers to use individual texts as entry points to preach on the lives of biblical characters in transition. Preachers can do this in one of two ways. On the one hand, we might tell the story of the biblical character's life as a journey of transition. For example, on the day when the lectionary appoints Ruth 1:6-18 as the first reading, I might relate Ruth's transition from ending to new beginning. In this instance, the verses that the congregation hears provide the kernel or essence of the story, one I would then relate more fully. Or I might relate different episodes from the character's life at different points in the congregation's transition. Elijah immediately comes to mind. I might tell the story of Elijah's victory over the prophets of Baal and God's gift of rain (1 Kings 18:17-46) as a positive change. Then, as the congregation struggles with the losses that come even with a positive change, I might preach on the way Jezebel's response turned Elijah's victory into an ending when she threatened the prophet's career (19:1-2). Elijah found himself in a liminal place as, fearing Jezebel, he fled for his life to Mount Horeb (19:3-18). Along the way, Elijah was nourished and sustained by God, who brought a new beginning in the call of Elisha (19:19-21). The story of Nicodemus is less dramatic. Nicodemus, who once came to Jesus by night (John 3:1-21), moves from skepticism to an in-between place. As the authorities conspire to have Jesus arrested, Nicodemus insists that they maintain an appropriate decision-making process (John 7:45-53). In the end, Nicodemus experiences an unanticipated new beginning as he boldly comes to the cross in the light of day to help Joseph of Arimathea prepare Jesus' body for burial (John 19:39).

Fourth, congregational transitions call preachers to consider who is "us" in the text. Justo and Catherine González observe: "Whenever we hear or read a narrative and seek to derive from it some meaning for ourselves, the message conveyed by the story depends in part on where we place ourselves in it."[13] We gain new insights and perspectives when we reassign the characters and take on different roles in the text. For example, people in different situations receive Jesus' parable of the Prodigal Son (Luke 15:11-32) differently. New Testament scholar Mark Powell observes that, while for many Americans this parable is about a greedy and ungrateful offspring, for people in other parts of the world it is about the devastating effects of a famine or the inability of a government to feed its people. Similarly, while we would never assume the role of either the landowner or the heir in Jesus' parable of the laborers in the vineyard (Luke 20:9-19), since those belong to God, we will experience the transition that occurs in this story differently, depending on whether we put ourselves in the place of the slaves or the tenants. The Gonzálezes caution us to avoid allegorizing when preaching on various roles in biblical narratives. Rather, we should take the concrete political situation in both the text and the congregation into account before assigning characters to contemporary people and circumstances.[14]

A fifth way that congregational transitions can shape our study of Scripture is for us to listen to some texts as though our ancestors in the faith, also in transition, were speaking directly to us. This method of studying Scripture consists of simply reading and then treating the text as if it were addressed to the preacher's congregation and transition.[15] As a veteran interim pastor completed her ministry, she effectively used words that Moses spoke to Joshua in the presence of Israel to address the congregation and the seminary graduate called to be its pastor: "Be strong and bold, for you are the one who will go with this people into the land that the Lord has sworn to their ancestors to give them; and you will put them in possession of it. It is the Lord who goes before you. He will be with you; he will not fail you or forsake you. Do not fear or be dismayed" (Deut. 31:7-8). While this method can be powerful and appropriate, it can also be dangerous and destructive. Before applying a Scripture quote directly to a congregations and its situation, a preacher must carefully exegete the text to determine that the text speaks to the present listeners in the same way that it spoke to its original listeners. When the preacher concludes that differences in time, place, circumstance, and audience blur or relativize the text's message, this approach should be avoided. In the Sermon on the Mount, for example, Jesus makes it plain that the words "Show no pity: life for life, eye for eye, tooth for tooth, hand for hand, foot for foot" (Deut. 19:21) should never be treated as a direct quotation from our ancestors (Matt. 5:28).

DETERMINE WHAT TO SAY

Studying Scripture through the lens of congregational transition yields a wealth of images, insights, perspectives, and potential messages. The preacher's next task is to determine the main point and purpose of the sermon from this plethora of possibilities. This step is undoubtedly the most challenging part of the process. At this point many preachers are given to pause or even to find themselves stalled because the layers, complexities, and emotional coloring of the transition make it hard to know exactly what to say. While God may occasionally speak so loudly and clearly that the preacher has no doubt about what needs to be said and heard, most often determining the central message of the transitional sermon is a matter of deliberation. If the message is too broad, God's Word may strike the congregation as vague and disconnected from the congregation, or God may seem intimidated by the change and transition. If the message is too narrow and precise, the sermon may dampen dialogue, silence differing perspectives, and alienate some members of the congregation.

Since the congregation, change, and transition are primary in preparing the transitional sermon, preachers need to know everything they can about the specific change, the dynamics of that transition, and what is happening in and with the congregation. In sermon preparation during a congregational transition, conversations about the change and transition with people both within and outside the congregation become more important. Preachers need to be open to hearing from as many people as possible because insight and wisdom can come from unexpected sources. Listening is so paramount to preparing and preaching the sermon in transition that I devote the next chapter to this task. For now, let us be clear that to determine the message of the sermon, preachers listen *to* the change, transition, congregation, and greater community. Preachers listen *for* the voice of preaching, the theological issues at stake, and the impact the transition has on the congregation and preacher. Readers feeling overwhelmed or stuck may choose to skip ahead to chapter 4 and return to this chapter when they have a better handle on the transition they are negotiating.

The goal in determining the message of the sermon is to formulate a "purpose statement" or a "focus statement." Ronald Allen observes that "one of the axioms of homiletics is that the preacher write a single sentence which summarizes the thrust of the sermon."[16] I like to think of the focus statement as a beacon that shines on everything—content, form, and style of delivery—that one considers including in the sermon. As a general rule, if the beacon is enhanced or reflected by whatever the preacher is considering, it is appropriate to the sermon; if the beacon is diminished or obscured, it is not. Allen notes that, at its best, the focus statement is a simple sentence that includes a subject, *action* verb, and predicate. It announces good news from God concerning God's love for the world and God's will for justice in the world. The subject of the sentence is normally "God," the verb is usually an activity of God, and the predicate is usually a benefit or consequence of God's love and justice. The tone is ordinarily positive, hopeful, and encouraging. Even when the congregation needs to be corrected, convicted, and challenged, the focus statement seeks to show how the gospel empowers the congregation to move beyond its limitations.[17]

The focus statement is always a declaration of good news. I join David Bartlett and many others in contending "that preaching is always good news. Preaching is news; it is fresh, involving, surprising. It is not the repetition of tired formulas or one more self-serving plug for [some] program. . . . It is always the herald's announcement of God's victory."[18] For Thomas Troeger, good news means that we "preach not answers but the living Christ."[19] According to Troeger, preaching the *living* Christ means proclaiming resurrection as more than the once-a-year theme of Easter. Christ's resurrection opens astonishing possibilities when we give up the delusion that we control reality. Resurrection is the vital ministry that results when a church releases its obsession with doing things as it has always done; resurrection is the future that opens to a society when it comes to terms with its prejudice and injustice. Resurrection is the vision of Christ that is granted us when we release the images we cling to in order to preserve what we hold dear and to feel secure.[20]

The good news is appropriate to the congregation and the transition. The preacher's task is to decide what about the gospel is new and good for the congregation in its situation. To speak to the community of faith, the preacher needs to be aware of all who make up the congregation: those who are using the transition to build themselves up and those whom the transition is tearing down, those speaking out and those keeping silent, those feeling responsible and those ready to blame. Some congregations may need to hear more about the freedom of the gospel, and other congregations may need to hear more about responsible living under the gospel.[21] But the preacher's task is always to discover and proclaim the gospel.

In times of congregational transition, the good news is determined in part by what people are thinking and saying. The gospel needs to be bold enough to name and address what people are thinking. The good news speaks *for* as well as *to* the congregation. In response to whatever the congregation is facing, the gospel assures the people of God's presence and gives them reason for hope. In this way, the sermon exhibits confidence in God. God is present all the time, but in times of transition, people look to the preacher to comment about *how* God is present. When the focus statement answers their question according to the gospel, the news is good.

CRAFT THE MANUSCRIPT

Once the preacher has determined the sermon's focus or central message, the next step is to craft the manuscript. While the shape or form of the sermon is based on its message or content, it is more than the packaging of that message. The shape or form is itself a way of getting the message heard. Fred Craddock describes the form of a sermon as "active, contributing to what the speaker wishes to say and do, sometimes no less persuasive than the content itself."[22] Ronald Allen writes, "When the form of the sermon is congruent with the purpose of the homily, the homily has a much better opportunity to accomplish its purpose than when form and purpose work against each other."[23] Pastors experienced at preaching in times of congregational transition amplify these professors' claims. They observe that confusion, anxiety, and uncertainty, which often characterize a time of congregational transition, can so diminish or even derail a message that carefully constructing the sermon becomes more important than arriving at the message, and delivering the sermon becomes more important than how it is shaped. During congregational transitions, the right message has a greater potential of being misheard or misinterpreted if it is said with the wrong words; the chances of this happening increase when the right words are said in the wrong way.

Fashioning the sermon is an attempt to take seriously both the gospel and the ways human beings order, understand, and appropriate reality.[24] As such, while there is no single established genre for sermons generally, a preacher can select from or modify distinct forms or structures in creating a particular sermon.[25] We are always free to imagine and create new forms for crafting homilies. Some preachers argue that framing the transition as a story or moving from the particular to the general makes the connection of the congregation's situation and God's story of salvation more accessible and apparent. For these preachers, a story sermon makes the message more memorable, helps people to see the situation in new ways, leads the congregation to imagine new possibilities and responses to its situation, and calls listeners to enter into an experience rather than receive information. Other preachers contend that a thematic approach to preaching—announcing the point of the sermon and then drawing out the implications in ways relevant to the congregation's situation—is the clearest way to bring the message home. This clarity can help the congregation feel secure and can offer an experience of orderliness amid the chaos of transition.

Ideally, the form the sermon takes flows naturally from the message. Unfortunately, at times the preacher knows what to say but not how to say it. When the content of the sermon does not make a form obvious, the preacher must carefully choose the form the sermon will take from established models—perhaps a story, a prophecy, a blessing, or three points. Generally, inspiring works better than directing; exploring is better than defining. When preachers need to select a sermon form, they should consider the congregation, the message, and the congregation's location in the transition. The primary audience for preaching in times of congregational transition is generally the faith community. The preacher therefore considers the forms of sermons that the congregation is accustomed to and even appreciates. While preachers do not automatically give the congregation what it wants, they recognize that introducing a new or unfamiliar sermon form introduces another variable into the preaching event. People may embrace or discount the message solely because of the form the sermon takes. The preacher also anticipates how the congregation feels about the message and how it will respond to the sermon. Laying out a theme and connecting it to the transition works best when the congregation agrees with the premise. Telling a story or moving from the particular to the general is a better approach when the sermon needs to change minds or move people to a different understanding and response. While the gathered congregation is the primary audience, preachers never lose track of who is overhearing the sermon. In crafting the sermon, preachers are mindful of as diverse of a community as possible so that the shape of the sermon aims to address and speak for everyone. This approach helps the sermon connect the congregation to the world and the transition to the congregation's mission.

The form of the sermon is also determined partly by where the congregation is in the transition. When the congregation is initially confronted by and coming to terms with change, preachers construct sermons in ways that paint the change as vividly as possible. It is important to be specific and to name the ripple effects, those second-, third-, and fourth-level changes that the initial change causes. The movement of the sermon leads the congregation from describing the situation to exploring and naming the change to identifying the problem that necessitates the transition. As the congregation's old identity and way of being is ending, the sermon is crafted in ways that bring losses out into the open, acknowledge them, and express concern, both God's and the congregation's, for those affected. When crafting the sermon during the ending strand, preachers carefully select words that name what is over and what is not. The tone of sermons preached during the ending strand shows respect for the past by articulating how endings ensure continuity with what really matters.

When the congregation is in the liminal strand of transition, one aim of the sermon is to clarify what the congregation needs to hang on to and what it needs to let go of. During the liminal strand, preachers have the important task of reminding the congregation that it cannot get back to normal—at all or too quickly—because there is no normal to get back to. As the congregation is reoriented and redirected in its life and identity, the sermon is shaped in ways that direct the congregation through chaos and confusion to God's unchanging love. During this time in the transition, it is helpful to proclaim freedom and forgiveness, the value that every member brings to the community, and patience with and trust in God.

As the congregation makes its new beginning, sermons are crafted to paint a vision that means something to the congregation. The vision connects the purpose the congregation seeks and God's purpose for the world. The vision also takes seriously both the risks the congregation is facing and the values it holds dear. Most important, the vision paints a picture of how the congregation will look and feel in its new reality and invites the members to become part of that picture.

Regardless of the phase of the transition, sermons are crafted differently during a long-term transition. Repeating and reminding is more important in long-term transitions; individual sermons can seek to accomplish less. For example, a long-term preaching strategy might be to "bookend" the transition by preaching a foundational sermon series at the beginning of the transition, referring to the transition throughout, and preaching a second sermon series at completion.

Finally, following Walter Brueggemann's lead, preachers might imagine crafting the transitional sermon as a river that consists of four currents: lamentation, assurance, promise, and invitation.[26] Each of these currents contributes to the sermon's flow and should be carefully considered in crafting the transitional sermon. Brueggemann reminds us that lamentation, the first current, calls us to "state what is happening by way of loss in vivid images so that the loss may be named by its right names and so that it can be publicly faced in the depth of its negativity."[27] Address the loss to God, who is implicated in it. Dare to give voice to the pain, loss, grief, shame, indignation, bewilderment, and rage that the congregation is feeling. Employ extreme images that cut through denial and self-deception. Although some preachers caution that we should not move through lament too quickly, others warn against wallowing there too long. A pastor in the Midwest, for example, encourages giving congregations ample time to name and experience their grief and loss so that these feelings are not minimized or denied. These preachers remind us of the powerful way that naming loss frees and empowers us to move ahead. One pastor declared, "Do not move too quickly to the good news! Stay with the congregation in their pain and loss so that their ears are wide open to the Gospel!" Rhashell Hunter, an African American Presbyterian minister, observes a difference in the black community as to how the preacher and the hearers approach transitional preaching. Instead of staying with lament, the African American preacher and congregation will move to celebration because amid loss, they have not lost everything. God is with them and loves them, so they celebrate.

Assurance, the second current, calls the preacher to assert that God is present to us, bringing newness out of seeming defeat. Brueggemann observes that we often "fail to notice what a daring act of faith such an utterance is, how blatantly it speaks against and beyond perceived circumstances in order to 'reconstruct, replace, or redraw the threatened paradigm of meaning.'"[28] Only by faith can the preacher speak and the congregation receive the assurance that God is not the prisoner of circumstance, that God can and will call into existence that which does not exist, so that both preacher and listeners anticipate what God is about to do.

The third current, promise, inspires the preacher to offer a vision of God's promised future, the future that will more fully embody God's intent for the congregation and, through the congregation, for the whole world. The picture of God's promised future is concrete, specific, local, and small. Most important, God's promised future is grounded in God, not in circumstance or in the congregation's efforts. Biblical images make a wonderful palette with which to create this image. For example, when I preached at a conference in a seminary chapel that had been gutted and was in the process of being remodeled, I used Ezra's description of Israel's return from Babylon to worship God in the demolished temple in Jerusalem (3:6-7). This portrait, along with the drilling, dust, chaos, and clutter of the seminary chapel, speaks of all of our spaces that, like the universe itself, are forever "under construction" as they continue to be formed and shaped by the hands of the Creator.

Finally, invitation, the fourth current, is the tone with which the preacher calls the congregation to abandon its despair and live the promise by entering into the journey of transition. When inviting people to respond, it is more effective to give examples than either abstractions or absolutes. When outlining the results of our efforts, it is more honest to identify possibilities rather than certitudes. Once again, be concrete, specific, local, and small when inviting people to respond so that they are eager and confident, rather than reluctant and overwhelmed.

While all four of these currents need to be considered in creating transitional sermons, the emphasis or primacy that each current is given in a particular sermon depends upon several factors, including the nature of the transition, where the pastor and congregation are in the transition, and the other processes occurring in the life of the congregation. After carefully considering these factors, the preacher may decide to leave one or more currents out of a sermon. The risk, of course, is that members of a congregation are seldom if ever emotionally in the same place. Even on a day of great celebration, some people in worship will have genuine cause to lament.

DELIVER THE SERMON

Once the manuscript is crafted, the preacher must consider how to deliver the sermon. A congregational transition affects sermon delivery in several ways. Sermon delivery encompasses everything that affects the preacher's ability to proclaim and the congregation's ability to receive the message.[29] Though sermon delivery is often assumed or overlooked in preparation, the benefits and risks of preaching in times of congregational transition make sermon delivery perhaps the most important aspect of the transitional sermon. The sermon's potential either to afford the congregation an experience of God's presence and grace or to divide and diminish the faith community, together with the urgency, uncertainty, and conflicting emotions that accompany a congregational transition, make it more likely for the message to be undermined or misinterpreted because of how something is said or how the preacher comes across.

The personality of the preacher affects both how the transitional sermon is delivered and how it is received, as well as how the congregation works its way through transition. The sermon's impact is affected by the preacher's attitude toward the transition, the congregation, the ministry, and the sermon. The transitional sermon will be shaped and delivered differently depending on whether the preacher approaches the change and transition as an opportunity or a threat. Some factors such as the pastor's age in relation to the average age of the congregation will also impinge on the preaching event. Although preachers need to take these factors into account, they are often beyond our control. Other aspects of the preacher's personality influence the preaching event in unpredictable ways. For example, Roman Catholic homiletician Walter J. Burghardt, S.J., contends that when the pastor is grieving preaching becomes more vulnerable and transparent. Burghardt asserts that when preachers are suffering servants, they are most strongly yoked to the Word of God and, therefore, preach best.[30] According to Burghardt, suffering charges our words with fresh power because we are uncommonly aware that of ourselves we can do nothing, that we must entrust our whole selves to the Lord, who alone can change hearts through our tongues. The congregation listens differently; it pulls for the preacher. A heightened emotional energy is evident. On the other hand, when preachers are not in control of their grief or when the content of the sermon becomes the expression of the preacher's grief, the message is lost as preaching is reduced to the pastor's personal therapy session.

Delivery is grounded in the pastoral relationship. Transition affects the relationship between the preacher and the congregation, in preaching and every other part of ministry. Some transitions enhance the preacher's authority to speak and the congregation's readiness to heed the message; other transitions diminish them. Preaching will be affected by factors such as the state of the pastoral relationship before the transition, whether the preacher is the cause of the change and transition, and whether the congregation and pastor share the same perspective or are on different sides of the issue. In times of transition, preachers need to remember that they are always change agents; we need to claim and embrace this role. At the same time, clergy can become the lightening rod in a transition, as can specific members of a congregation. Finally, preaching is enhanced when the congregation experiences consistency in what the preacher proclaims and the quality of the preacher's life, particularly the way he or she leads the congregation through transition. For example, the preacher cannot invite the congregation to participate in a decision-making process and then unilaterally make and announce decisions.

As for practical suggestions for delivering the transitional sermon, disregard any notion that when the sermon is written it is complete. Spend more time preparing your delivery and rehearsing your sermons, since how something is said is extremely important in this kind of preaching. The goal is to become so familiar with the sermon that it is in your very being and you can hear the way the sermon comes out of you. This kind of preparation increases confidence as well as effectiveness.

Strive to be playful rather than solemn in the delivery. Rather than being rational, dare to dream. Offer possibility rather than platitude. Be unfolding as opposed to final. Rather than scold, tease and invite. Be serious as opposed to morbid; present and embodied, not artificial and detached. The delivery should not appear well rehearsed. Instead, at its best this preaching invites the hearers to experience an utterance not available until the very moment it is said. In this way, the intersection of gospel and transition is birthed. It is surprise. Obviously, for this to happen, the preacher must be well prepared.

Delivery takes seriously the members of the congregation and their place in the transition. Preachers shape delivery according to whether the transition has a major or a minor effect on the congregation. They consider who is at the heart of the transition and who is at the periphery. They are mindful of which people are concerned with "winning" or being elevated in power and status, and which people are losing power and status or being alienated. Preachers also consider people's feelings and perspectives. Since everyone is touched differently by change and transition, the preacher anticipates and remains alert to the ways people are affected in worship. Preachers notice whether there is a buzz in the congregation as people gather for worship. They consider what they are hearing about the issue, and what people are discussing with each other. Preachers notice who is in worship and who is missing. They are attuned to whether people are taking sides. Thus, the sermon is nuanced—it might even change slightly between the first service and the second.

Finally, the preacher considers the space in which preaching occurs because the space itself has the power either to enhance or to detract from effective sermon delivery. During a congregational transition, when emotions are already running high, the feelings and memories that the faith community associates with the worship space affect preaching by the influence they exert on both the listeners and the preacher. Preachers take these feelings and memories into account. Preachers might also consider whether to use the pulpit or preach from the aisle. While for some leaving the pulpit might be received as standing among the people, for others it might signal the preacher's abandoning the authority of God's Word. Thus, congregational expectations, as well as the preacher's preparedness, comfort, and sense of authority, and the message and the occasion all contribute to this decision.

In this chapter, I have identified the ways a congregational transition influences the process of sermon preparation. I also outlined the decisions and choices the preacher needs to make in preparing the transitional sermon. As I worked through the process of selecting and studying Scripture, determining the message, crafting the manuscript, and delivering the sermon, I repeatedly asserted the pivotal roles that the congregation, the transition, and the preacher's own feelings and perceptions play in preaching through a congregational transition. In the next chapter, I explore how the preacher listens to these voices as an essential part of preparing and preaching the transitional sermon.

Questions for Reflection

- What is your method of sermon preparation and delivery?
- How is your method working? What about it do you affirm? What about it might you like to rethink or change? Do you trust God to work in and through your weekly routine?
- How do you select Scripture for preaching? Do you use a lectionary or a topical approach? On what occasions have you veered from this routine?
- How has the transition changed your normal method of sermon preparation? How do you evaluate these changes?

CHAPTER 4

HOLY AND ACTIVE LISTENING

When preachers who have led congregations through significant transitions were asked what they wished they had known or done before attempting to preach through a congregational transition, one pastor answered, "I wish I'd had a map that showed me the pitfalls. I needed to do more to become better informed about what I was getting into." Another pastor replied, "I wish I'd have asked more questions of people on the outside going in, especially before climbing into the pulpit." Over and over, preachers reinforced the vital role that listening plays in preaching through a congregational transition. By carefully listening, preachers determine how to make the most of the benefits while avoiding the risks of preaching through transition in any given sermon. The goal is to learn as much as possible about the nature of the change and transition; the congregation or faith community; the role of preaching in the life of that congregation; the surrounding community or greater context; the theological or faith issues at stake; and the preacher's own biases, perspective, and comfort level. In chapter 2 I discussed using "listening posts" that inform preaching. Listening posts include conversations that naturally emerge in the course of pastoral ministry, the activities of congregational life, and the mechanisms especially established in response to the transition, including the monitoring team. In this chapter I explore how to listen to and include these voices in the preparation and preaching of the transitional sermon.

Listening is the primary and essential way that pastors plumb the depths of the lives of people both within the congregation and in the greater community.[1] In pastoral ministry listening is a given; pastors are expected to be good listeners. In a congregational transition, when there is much to consider, communicate, decide, and do, leaders may be tempted to under-estimate the extraordinary value of listening. After all, listening is such an ordinary thing. Leaders often need to remind themselves that, when we spend time listening, we are doing something indispensable to leading the transition. Listening is key to preaching and leading a congregation through transition for several reasons. First, while many resources like this book aim at helping pastors and congregations make their way through change and transition, any plan needs to be put in the congregation's context. Re-gardless of where a congregation finds itself on the journey of transition, the specific steps that it takes must be tailored in ways that are often hard to determine. Listening helps leaders and congregations adjust the pattern so that it fits the congregation. Listening also keeps people from shutting down, withdrawing, and distancing themselves because they do not feel heard and valued. Considered another way, listening fosters a stronger bond among the congregation's members, a unity of spirit in the community of faith, and a willingness to risk and disclose the self. At its best, listening creates trust as people share experiences and ideas and come to realize that they also share values, desires, and dreams.

Listening in times of congregational transition is active. Together with other leaders, preachers listen to people's words; they also listen for "holy screams for new life, or sighs too deep for words."[2] That is to say, preachers listen for what is said beneath the surface and beyond the obvious. An ac-tive listener invites the person speaking to say more about what he or she is thinking and feeling without attempting to steer or close off the conversa-tion. This kind of listening requires preachers and other leaders to be pre-pared to listen to people at length and in depth and not to be content with merely listening long enough to frame a problem and formulate a solution. The preacher's goal, in fact, is to cultivate a habit of deliberately listening to every aspect and activity of human life—individual lives, the life of the congregation, and the preacher's own life. This kind of active listening takes skill and practice. It involves expressing interest through caring behavior, using appropriate facial expressions and posture, posing open-ended ques-tions, and closely observing nonverbal cues. Active listening depends on the listener's ability to paraphrase, clarify, probe, comprehend, confront, and sort all that the listener receives. Active listening calls for courage; it asks us to be willing to hear things that startle the teller, the listener, or both. Active listeners are natural; they do not appear to be performing a skill; they are authentic and do not seem rehearsed. Active listeners remain patient and approachable. Active listeners also give attention to physical place and emotional space so that people feel welcome and safe.

Yet, more than active, *listening in times of congregational transition is holy*. It demands that we engage in listening to discover the presence and activity of God in the joys, struggles, and hopes of the ordinary activities of congregational life, as well as the uncertainty and opportunity of change and transition. Listening is holy because, during a transition, we expect to hear the voice, presence, or absence of God. Holy listening demands vigilance, alertness, openness to others, and the expectation that God will speak through them. Holy listening trusts that the Holy Spirit acts in and through our listening. We discern and discover the wisdom and will of God by listening to one another and to ourselves. From a Christian perspective, holy listening also takes the incarnation seriously; it dares to believe that, as God was enfleshed in Jesus of Nazareth, so God is embodied in other people and in the things around us. By expecting God to speak in and through the congregation itself, holy listening prevents us from searching so hard for an extraordinary and miraculous epiphany that we miss God with us. Holy listening also reminds both preacher and congregation that they are valued children of God, called and gifted to attend to what is meaningful to God's life and work in the world.

Holy and active listening is multifaceted. Holy and active listening demands many venues and numerous means of listening so that all voices are heard. It occurs in the ordinary and routine tasks of ministry when pastors are attentive to both their own and others' yearnings, weariness, questions, and supplications. It occurs in the fellowship, worship, and celebrations of congregational life when people spontaneously share their joy, excitement, convictions, and thanksgivings. In times of congregational transition, holy and active listening is practiced more overtly, using the processes, occasions, and mechanisms the congregation establishes to manage and monitor the transition. Preachers should be alert to the possibility that any encounter, conversation, gathering, or meeting might prove to be an opportunity to hear and learn something vital. As previously indicated, people may not say anything directly or outright. Therefore, preachers often listen best by observing, overhearing, and being attuned to people's feelings and the mood of the room. Preachers sometimes listen best by inviting someone else to ask the questions. Determining the best ways and places to listen is tiring work. Remaining open to all voices, opinions, emotions, and reactions is even more exhausting. Listening to everyone includes listening to those who say things about the pastor and congregation that are difficult to hear and might even be untrue. It involves listening to people who question motives, have their own agendas, and understand their role to be obstruction.

For this reason, *holy and active listening is imperfect.* Our listening is influenced by our own needs, feelings, aspirations, experiences, and preconceptions. Our listening is influenced by what we do not want to hear because sometimes we do not want to change our understanding and undertake the subsequent changes in either our ministry or the congregation that a new understanding would lead to. We may be tempted to listen for reality as we would like it rather than for the way things actually are. We might find ourselves listening to confirm what we already think rather than remaining open to being surprised by others, to God speaking through others, or to the discovery of something new. Obviously, our listening is influenced by the questions we ask. A congregational leader once gathered inactive members to ask, "What is it about our pastor that keeps you from being active in church?" That leader's assumption was obvious. As important as the way we ask questions are the questions we do not ask. For example, how often do we invite people to name the ways they experience God's presence in the congregation, or to identify the grace of God at work in the congregation? Finally, as we listen, we may be distracted or preoccupied by what we will do next. We might move too quickly to solve rather than hear problems.

Pastors who consciously reflect upon listening when a congregation is in transition tell us that *the work of holy and active listening is overwhelming.* The size of the task, its intensity, and the recognition that pastors will miss something or someone, however hard they try, often leave pastors feeling inadequate, incapable, and deluged with work. These colleagues remind us that listening is not an additional task, but something pastors are already doing as part of their ministry. They emphasize that God not only speaks as we listen; God helps us to listen. They assure us that, more than a means of determining how to preach and lead a congregation through transition, holy and active listening is itself an act of proclamation and leadership.

Though imperfect and overwhelming, holy and active listening is above all else essential when preaching through a congregational transition. While pastors must develop their own skills and style of listening, we can consider whom to listen to and what to listen for. In times of congregational transition, preachers need to hear the voices of the change and transition, the congregation, the role of preaching, the theological issues at stake, and the inner life of the preacher. Now I turn to considering how each of these voices can help strengthen this essential part of ministry.

THE CHANGE AND TRANSITION

Since the change that necessitates the transition and the transition itself both impinge on how one preaches through the transition, preachers should listen carefully to the change and continue to listen to the transition. Unfortunately, preachers sometimes listen well as the change occurs but listen less as the transition progresses. Mindful that the goal of preaching through a congregational transition is to understand and interpret the change and transition in light of the gospel, the preacher needs to possess a thorough knowledge of both. Preaching can easily be undone if the preacher is perceived as uninformed, oversimplifying, misrepresenting, stereotyping, and even unintentionally distorting the truth. Only by accurately comprehending the change and transition can the preacher help the congregation understand the change and transition in light of the gospel and respond in faith.

Asked how to begin the important work of listening, one pastor replied, "Learn all you can about the change." Before assessing, analyzing, and concluding, preachers must obtain all the factual information that they can. Double- and triple-checking is appropriate. Hearing every side of an issue generates goodwill as well as a more balanced perspective. When preachers are ready to analyze and assess the information they have gathered, they should do so out of their theological expertise. Scripture, doctrine, church history, and the denomination's theological and social statements or positions are among the evaluative tools that the preacher employs.

In addition to assessing the situation using the resources of their faith tradition, preachers should avail themselves of the expertise of the natural and social sciences to learn as much as they can about the particular change and transition. When, for example, a congregation found its property affected by a toxic spill from a neighboring manufacturing plant, the pastor found herself immersed in environmental impact statements. Besides spending time in the library or bookstore, the preacher might enlist the advice and counsel of experts, both within and outside the congregation. At the very least, preachers will carefully read the newspaper, watch the evening news, or spend some time on the Internet. One preacher observed that the context increases so much in importance when preaching through a congregational transition that reading the newspaper and going to the library become more essential than exegesis.

Ronald Allen suggests that preachers make a list of everything they need to know about a topic to discuss it intelligently. From Allen's perspective, this list most surely includes the origin and history of the change and transition, its current manifestation and all the issues related to it, and theological resources with which to understand and evaluate the change and transition.[3] Colleagues suggest that describing the change and transition categorically also produces helpful insights. I discussed in chapter 1 the nature of change using such categories as public, congregational, and personal; originating outside or within the congregation; unexpected or anticipated; traumatic or subtle; and unpredictable or a natural part of congregational life. These descriptors are helpful as preachers sort out all that they are hearing. In the second section of this book, I offer "briefs" on transitions that result from eight changes that may occur in the life of a congregation. Understanding a *brief* as a summary, these reflections are intended to whet rather than satisfy the preacher's appetite for information and understanding.

In considering the change, it is important to determine whether the change will, in fact, cause a *congregational* transition. Important changes in the lives of members, the community, and even the congregation can initiate transitions that have only a minimal impact on the congregation. When a company in town announced layoffs, the congregational board was ready to cut parish programs and slash the congregation's budget. When the pastor calmly inquired about the number of families in the congregation that would be affected by the layoffs, the answer was "one." The importance attributed to this change to the life of the congregation quickly diminished. Rather than worrying about its own future, the congregation concentrated on the affected family. Our response to these sorts of changes and transitions will differ greatly from the way we respond to transitions that strike the congregation deeply and directly. Recognizing the prominence that congregations accord an issue that is addressed from the pulpit, preachers need to determine whether the change and transition are of sufficient weight to be included in preaching. David Buttrick observes, "Nothing is more embarrassing than a pulpit addressing questions that no one asks, or that are asked but are trivial."[4] Preachers must also remain attuned to the fact that changes they do not consider significant enough for preaching may be important to the congregation. The guest preacher of a congregation celebrating a significant anniversary the weekend Ronald Reagan died did not mention the former president's death in the sermon. Some parishioners were outraged. Of course, a preacher may decide that the very nature of a change or transition makes it worthy or unworthy of preaching, independent of what the congregation thinks.

The degree to which the congregation perceives the change and transition as traumatic is a second factor that helps determine how one preaches through the transition. Some pastors argue that, the more traumatic the transition, the more direct and delicate the preaching needs to be. Asking where the congregation would place the news of the change on a scale from problem to opportunity is a simple way of gauging trauma. A second approach might be to consider how close the change is to the congregation's heart. Stated another way, preachers might listen for how deeply and broadly the congregation is affected. A third approach to assessing trauma is to listen for clues about how raw the change leaves particular members of the congregation—a board member, a member who is homebound, a Sunday school teacher, a youth, an inactive member. This approach helps pastors and congregations expand their understanding of the change and transition, and to develop empathy for the various ways people are affected. In assessing how traumatic a transition is, it is important to name all the transitions that a change will bring. The preacher might then gauge the degree of trauma by counting the number of transitions that will occur, identifying the one that is most difficult, and determining how difficult that transition will be.

Listening for the extent to which the change and transition are public also helps determine how one preaches through the transition. Some changes and transitions are so public and traumatic that preachers do not have the freedom to refrain from speaking or to be guarded in what they say because people want a direct comment from one who speaks for God. When change and transition are less than public, leaders need to determine what, if anything, the congregation must be told. In these circumstances, it is essential to distinguish between disclosing information and preaching through the transition. The pulpit is generally not the best place to disclose information without comment or reflection. In fact, a congregational leader other than the pastor may be the better choice for carrying out this responsibility. Making these determinations involves identifying the boundaries and levels of disclosure and self-disclosure in the change and transition. In transitions, boundaries are difficult to identify but essential to maintain. Clergy need to ask themselves, Who needs to know what? What do I need to do alone? What do leaders and members need to know and be part of? Leaders must decide what and how much is necessary and permissible to share. Who in the congregation needs to know and do what?

The timing of the change and transition is another factor to be considered. Preachers should consider both the timing of the change and transition in general and the timing of the change in relation to the next preaching event in particular. Some changes and transitions are sudden and unexpected, while others are slow and anticipated. Some transitions are acute, demanding immediate comment; others are long-term, offering many occasions for preaching. To respond appropriately to some changes and transitions, the pastor and congregational leaders need time to gather information, or the congregation needs time to absorb the reality. In these instances, preaching through the transition might best be delayed. A third consideration related to timing is whether members of the congregation will hear about the change and transition from another source or through the grapevine and imagine and fear the worst. The risk of delay and avoidance, even in the short run, is that these approaches might engender anger, suspicion, and ill will. Bridges asserts that "for every week of delay, you gain a month of bitterness and mistrust."[5]

THE CONGREGATION

While it may seem obvious that preachers should listen to the congregation in a congregational transition, the members are sometimes discounted as uninformed, incapable of grasping either the theological significance of a change and transition or the big picture, or so entrenched in old identity and behavior that they are unwilling to think in new ways. These conclusions also discount the power of God at work in the congregation. Preachers therefore need to resist the temptation to discount or dismiss. Rather, they need to listen seriously to their congregations, using the skills discussed at the beginning of this chapter.

Listening to the congregation's board and other leaders is a good way to start. The pastor will also naturally encounter members who regularly participate in worship and are active in the congregation's life. Listening to people on the fringes and inactive members takes extra effort. In some situations, such as when a change involves an entire community, preachers may want to be in conversation with colleagues and members of neighboring congregations. While some pastors urge consulting church judicatories (presbytery, synod, conference, diocese) in these conversations, other pastors caution that the advice and perceptions offered by church judicatories are often dated and slanted to support the judicatory's agenda. In all fairness, both statements are true. Some judicatories have teams of people trained to help congregations deal with specific transitions, such as pastoral changes or betrayals of trust. While church judicatories can provide helpful insights and direction, they have their own interests and agenda and are often only periodically in direct contact with a particular congregation.

The overall health of the congregation also determines the way the transition is managed, including the way the transition is addressed in preaching. Preachers therefore listen carefully to the congregation to understand its culture. Ideally, a pastor has been learning about the congregation's culture since before he or she began serving the congregation. Of particular importance, a preacher should listen for how the congregation understands its ministry, deals with conflict, and has managed previous transitions. These all affect both how the congregation manages the current transition and the place of preaching in that process. Is the congregation's life together open and healthy, or conflicted? Does the congregation understand its ministry as an ongoing transition or view its life as stable and unchanged? How does the congregation deal with conflict? What are the congregational norms? In a congregation that understands its ministry as a journey, one that views conflict as the means by which the Spirit works in its midst, preaching through a transition will be freer and more direct than in a congregation that does its best to maintain the status quo and to avoid conflict at all costs.

The preacher will also want to listen for what the congregation thinks and how its members feel about the change and transition. People may not communicate their thoughts and feelings directly. As in pastoral conversation generally, the preacher may need to uncover these reactions as parishioners relate their experience of the change and transition. Congregational documents prepared by members, including annual reports, meeting minutes, and newsletter articles may also prove helpful here. Of course, members of a congregation rarely all have the same experience of a change and transition, let alone think and feel the same way about it. Ronald Allen suggests, however, "Even diverse bodies have a center of gravity where a significant body of the congregation's experience can be taken into account."[6] Preachers listen to the congregation to discover this center of gravity without dismissing those who weigh the situation differently.

Preachers should listen for and anticipate the ways the identity, attitudes, and behavior of the congregation and its members will need to change because of the transition. Specifically, what will the members of the congregation need to stop doing and what will they need to start doing? Preachers should strive to determine who stands to lose what in the transition and exactly what they must let go of. In making these determinations, preachers pay attention to more than people's responsibilities and tasks. Preachers are also attuned to the ways the attitudes, roles, and identities that shape people's inner world need to change. In a congregation where a pastor in his 60s was followed by a pastor in his 30s, members who had for years served as the first pastor's "kitchen cabinet" became a vocal opposition when the new pastor naturally gravitated to people his own age and the "kitchen cabinet" moved to the "kids' table." Rather than opposing the changes the pastor was making, the older members resented their loss of role and status. The preacher should also listen for losses the entire congregation is experiencing. The preacher should be attentive to whether the congregation views these losses as symbolic of a greater loss or as the first step in a series of losses. The move from one to two worship services is an obvious example of what many people regard as the first loss in a series of losses. The schedule of every member of the congregation is changed. For some members of the congregation, this change brings the loss of relationships as people choose different services. For others, the loss is even greater as the congregation's identity as a flock gives way to a herd with more than one flock.

Besides listening for the ways the congregation's identity, attitudes, and behavior will need to change, preachers also need to listen for the immediacy, nature, and extent of these changes because these also influence how the transition is addressed in preaching. For example, large and immediate changes often need to be addressed directly and immediately in preaching. In measuring the impact of the transition on the congregation, preachers seriously anticipate the level of "overreaction." Preachers need to listen carefully to people's feelings and to weigh the probable manifestations and intensity of the congregation's "overreaction," rather than allowing themselves to be surprised by it. As they do when assessing other aspects of response to change, preachers can estimate the congregation's "overreaction" by calculating the losses brought on by the change, the past losses the congregation has experienced, and the ways the congregation dealt with change in the past. One pastor observed, "I assume that everyone is wounded in congregational transitions. My job is to find out how and how much."

The congregation's level of "transition fatigue" also affects both its current culture and its likely reaction and overreaction to subsequent change and transition. Previously I defined *transition fatigue* as the weariness and resistance that often result from the piling up of many transitions, one on another. Obviously, the higher the level of transition fatigue, the more likely it is that the congregation will experience the transition as traumatic and overreact to the change. It is essential to recognize that various segments of the congregation may differ in their levels of transition fatigue. Elected leaders and staff, for example, will most likely have a higher level of transition fatigue than those whose involvement in the congregation is confined to Sunday worship. It is also important to consider the added transition fatigue that may result from change and transition in areas of life beyond the congregation. Life outside church may cause people to be traumatized by and to overreact to change and transition within the congregation, particularly if they have relied on their community of faith as a place of stability and certitude in the midst of change and upheaval.

Finally, while every member of the congregation needs to be heard during a congregational transition, and while certain individuals and groups, such as the congregational board or council, will be heard more than others, two groups within the congregation deserve special attention— (1) visitors and (2) members with whom the preacher has been in conflict. When preaching in times of congregational transition, the preacher pastorally attends and listens to those with whom he or she is in conflict. In determining how to preach through the transition, the preacher needs to try to identify those people and formulate an appropriate pastoral response in advance of preaching. When possible, the best way to do this is to hear their views and concerns and together find ways to address them. Pastors reach out both to people who disagree with them and to people with whom they disagree. In addition to those with whom the preacher may experience conflict in the current transition, the preacher should attend to those with whom she or he has a history of conflict. It is also important to note that, in times of transition, alliances tend to change quickly and unpredictably. Listening for issues of power is therefore most important. At times, people question, object, and disagree with the pastor to preserve relationships or to maintain or enhance their power and status. In these instances, answering questions, addressing objections, and empowering people to speak will not prove effective. When listening to those who disagree with the pastor, both pastors and congregational leaders should be aware that in times of transition it is easy to get sidetracked by victims, especially by what one pastor termed the congregation's "professional victims"—those whose role in the congregation is to blame, complain, feel hurt, feel ignored, and stand in the way. In these instances, the appropriate pastoral response may be the willingness to live with conflict, rather than accommodation.

From listening to visitors, the preacher will gain information that may not be available from any other source—for example, how the congregation is perceived in the community. Visitors, who are not necessarily caught up in the transition and may not even be aware of it, are perhaps in the best position to alert the pastor when the transition overshadows the gospel in either the sermon or the congregation's life. A visitor to one congregation suggested that the congregation not publish weekly giving statistics in the Sunday bulletin because the deficit scared people away. During a pastoral vacancy in another congregation, while members fretted over lack of leadership and direction, visitors joined the church because they experienced people struggling in a positive way to own the ministry. While suggestions and observations like these may not be immediately forthcoming, when pastors and other leaders get in touch with visitors to learn either what about the congregation keeps them coming or what about the congregation leads them to continue their search for a church home, visitors will share important perspectives. Listening to visitors also helps to guarantee that the congregation's concern is for their spiritual well-being. Visitors come to worship seeking an experience of God and hoping to receive the grace of the gospel. Unfortunately, congregations sometimes view visitors as resources or solutions to congregational problems. This perspective is best exemplified in one congregation's "Full Pews Mean Full Plates" evangelism campaign, in which increased membership was hailed as the best way to solve the congregation's budgetary crisis.

THE ROLE OF PREACHING

When listening to the congregation, preachers should listen in particular for the role that preaching plays in the life of the congregation. The more the congregation regards preaching as central to its life, the more likely the congregation is to turn to the pulpit when confronted by change and transition. One indication of the place of preaching in the life of a congregation may be the amount of time the pastor spends in sermon preparation and preaching during a typical week of ministry. Though there are exceptions to the rule, congregations that have a high regard for preaching generally expect their pastor to devote considerable time and energy to sermon preparation and delivery. Another indication may be the degree to which the congregation perceives that its preaching ministry connects to its real life. When preaching regularly brings the gospel to bear on the issues and events confronting individuals, the church, the community, the nation, and the world, people will expect preaching to bring the gospel to bear on the issues and events confronting the congregation.

Asking the people in the pews what they think about preaching is often the best way to determine its place in their lives and in the life of the congregation. Inasmuch as pastors have a personal stake in the preaching ministry, they are sometimes least able to assess it objectively, either because they cannot see the inadequacy of their own preaching or because humility prevents them from acknowledging the profound impact their preaching has on the lives of their congregants. Rather than (or perhaps in addition to) pastors themselves asking individuals about preaching, mechanisms should be employed to ensure objectivity. Whether in individual interviews conducted by someone other than the pastor, in small groups, or through a questionnaire or survey, parishioners could be asked, "What difference does the Sunday sermon make to your life during the week?" The question becomes all the more effective when, immediately after worship, members of the congregation are asked, "What difference will this sermon make in your life in the coming week?" The congregation might also be asked, "How likely are you to turn to your pastor's preaching when you experience change or crisis?" Questions like these should be asked only if the pastor and leadership are genuinely interested in what the members of the congregation have to say and if it is truly safe for them to give an honest answer.

The way a pastor preaches in times of congregational transition also depends on whether the congregation trusts the pulpit. Inasmuch as preaching is so relational, congregations are more likely to trust preaching when a strong bond of trust links the listeners and the preacher. The congregation's level of trust is enhanced when the pastor uses preaching to prepare the congregation for change and transition so that the pulpit becomes the place from which parishioners expect to receive assurance, orientation, direction, and meaning. This trust also depends on how the congregation's pastors have historically addressed transitions from the pulpit. If the pulpit has been used to force a single agenda, with the preacher clubbing the congregation with Scripture to drive that agenda home, preaching will be a less effective way to address the transition. On the other hand, if preaching regularly proclaims the ever-expanding love of God as revealed in the living Christ, which shatters both our expectations and everything we think will last, the congregation will be better prepared for change and more open to encounter God in preaching amid transition. Preachers should therefore listen carefully for clues to how people have experienced preaching in the past. Finally, as I discussed in chapter 2, the role that preaching plays during a congregational transition is enhanced when the congregation experiences strong collaboration and consistency between preaching and the other processes used to lead the transition.

THE THEOLOGICAL ISSUE AT STAKE

In all of their interactions, preachers must listen carefully to hear what theological or faith issue is at stake in the change and transition. As they sift through everything they hear, preachers should ask, What question about God is the congregation asking? What meaning about God is being generated? People may assign different, even contradictory, theological meaning to a given situation. For example, a youth pastor confronted by abuse and addiction in the lives of the young people she served railed against God for doing nothing to help; at the same time, the congregation praised God for sending a pastor who was making a profound difference in young people's lives. The preacher's purpose when listening theologically is to determine the best way to help people make theological "sense" of the transition and to find the right words with which to articulate what the change and transition "mean" for our relationship with God. By using these words from the pulpit, the preacher gives these words to the congregation.

Analyzing the transition with a credible theological method helps preachers understand and address the faith questions that are asked and the theological meaning that is assigned. In chapter 1, I talked about change causing people a crisis of understanding, a crisis of decision, or both. David Buttrick speaks of "limit moments or decision moments."[7] Buttrick describes *limit moments* as those "characterized by a sudden awareness of transcendent mystery and, at the same time, acknowledgment of our human finitude."[8] In these moments we are aware that the world in which we live is inadequate and that a bigger, more mysterious world surrounds us. Then we seek new understanding. In *decision moments* we are forced to consider seriously a course of action. In these moments impulses and conventions are in conflict, and precedents are simply not available. People agonize over decisions because risks are high and outcomes are uncertain. How and what they decide communicates something of their identity to themselves and to others. In these moments, people seek either direction or a framework for making their own decision.

Ronald Allen suggests three theological criteria that preachers might apply to the change and transition.[9] First, are the ways that people understand and respond to the change and transition *appropriate to the gospel*? Put another way, do the ways that people understand and respond to the change and transition manifest God's unconditional love and justice for all? Second, are the ways that people understand and respond to the change and transition *intelligible*? Do they make sense in terms of both what the congregation believes and the way the congregation understands and views the world? While Allen labels this criterion "intelligibility," it may be helpful to understand this criterion as *consistency*. Are the ways people understand and respond consistent with their faith and worldview? Allen calls his third criterion *moral plausibility*. This criterion asks the preacher to consider whether the congregation's understanding and response exhibit God's love for everyone in the situation, including all of creation, and God's work of bringing justice for all. Allen observes that these criteria overlap, but each has its own accent.

In addition to the approaches we have outlined, preachers might engage in dialogue with the writings of a favorite theologian, consider the change and transition using a specific doctrine, explore church history for a helpful precedent, or ask how the church's liturgy and sacraments inform the change and transition. Regardless of the theological tools that a preacher uses, the preacher's method must be sound. The preacher must understand that change and transition may shake the congregation's faith and invite the congregation to question God.

THE PREACHER'S INNER WORLD

For preachers, listening to themselves, to their inner world, is as important as listening to others. Their theological expertise, faith perspective, ministry experience, hunches, and instincts are invaluable resources for preaching in times of congregational transition. In addition to these assets, preachers also listen for their own biases and feelings about the change and transition because these, too, influence how the preacher understands the change and leads the congregation. This influence is especially strong in preaching, which by its very nature is inseparable from the person of the preacher. When preachers listen for their biases and emotions, they can decide whether to heed or ignore them. Left unexamined, these personal prejudices and persuasions may reveal themselves in preaching in ways the preacher neither anticipates nor endorses. Throughout the change and transition, preachers will therefore regularly and mindfully cultivate and reflect upon their emotions, memories, images, impressions, thoughts, convictions, questions, and decisions. Turning off the internal sensor or editor is key to truly listening to one's inner world and discovering what one is thinking, feeling, and experiencing.

Ronald Allen provides several tools to help preachers listen to their inner selves.[10] He invites preachers to associate freely to the change and transition and then examine their free associations for patterns, particularly patterns that will affect preaching. Allen asks preachers to consider what images form in their minds and what these images reveal about their orientation toward the change and transition. Some pastors take this strategy a step farther and find it helpful to track the images that appear in their dreams. Preachers will obviously want to identify the feelings they experience as they consider the change and lead the congregation through the transition and reflect on how these feelings predispose them. Preachers will also work to formulate and articulate their questions and convictions. Allen also calls preachers to discover areas of the change and transition they do not understand, things about it that rub them the wrong way, and the degree to which they truly care about the change, the transition, and the outcome.

Preachers should listen attentively for their comfort level, the way they understand their role as pastor, and their underlying assumptions about areas of life related to the transition. How pastors preach depends, in part, on how comfortable they feel in and about the transition. As I have said, the preacher's comfort level is influenced by many factors, including the nature of the congregation and the transition, the preacher's perspectives and how they match the congregation's perspectives, the urgency and sense of trauma that the situation creates, and the faith questions that the preacher and congregation are asking.

Preachers also need to account for those aspects of the change and transition that relate to them directly. A congregational transition often initiates a transition in the life of the preacher. While personal and congregational transitions can overlap, they are, in reality, distinct. For example, in response to the same congregational transition, pastors may question their leadership skills, consider whether it is time for a change in their ministry context, or find themselves excited to be shaken out of long-established routines. For some preachers, personal transitions touch them so deeply that it becomes difficult for them to preach. For other preachers, personal transitions empower and energize to the point that these sermons are among their most faithful and effective. Still other pastors find it impossible to separate their own identity from that of the congregation. Self-awareness is key to distinguishing and understanding personal and congregational transitions. It is also important for pastors to exhibit congruence between the way they understand, respond to, and manage their personal transition, and the way they lead and ask others to participate in the congregational transition. It is hard, for example, for pastors to ask the congregation to risk and step boldly in faith as they seek personal security for themselves. At the same time, pastors cannot ignore the fact that they and their families may be at personal risk because of congregational change and transition. Pastors may become so unpopular that they find themselves ignored, isolated, and the object of rumor and gossip. Preachers may even risk losing their position and their employment. These risks will certainly raise a preacher's anxiety about preaching through a transition.

How pastors preach through a congregational transition also depends on how pastors understand their place and role in the transitional process. Increasingly, both pastors and congregations understand a key part of the pastoral role to be dealing with transition. One pastor observed, "If change isn't imposed from without, clergy need to bring it about from within." Pastors need to consider carefully their personal approach to conflict because the way they deal with conflict will affect their preaching. A pastor who welcomes and cultivates conflict will approach preaching differently from a pastor who seeks to avoid conflict at all costs.

Many pastors report that, especially during change and transition, congregations tend to look up to clergy and fail to recognize that their pastor is also affected by transitions. Pastors should therefore remain aware of how they are feeling about the "pastoral pedestal" or, conversely, about being "dethroned." They should also be keenly aware that in some transitions the pastoral office is violated and their capacity to preach is diminished. Such a situation most likely results from a boundary violation; however, the pastoral office is also violated in less dramatic ways. Pastors announcing that they have accepted another appointment or call are in a sense betraying the people they serve. Even pastoral accomplishments such as increasing the congregation's membership will be viewed by some as the pastor's shirking of responsibilities to long-term members for the sake of the new people. Pastors need to acknowledge and remedy actual violations of the pastoral office and find ways to deal constructively with congregational disappointment that takes the form of accusation and criticism of their ministry. I will have much more to say on this topic in chapter 5. Pastors should also be aware that their capacity to preach may be diminished by the congregation's experience of other pastors who acted irresponsibly either within or outside the preaching role.

Our assumptions affect everything we do, including preaching. Preachers therefore need to be aware of their theological assumptions, such as how they understand that God is at work in change. Preachers should also be mindful of their socioeconomic and political assumptions. Two pastors approached layoffs in opposite ways because of their assumptions. The first pastor, a strong advocate for God's preferential treatment of the poor, was firmly on the side of the employees. This pastor was raised in a blue-collar home. The other pastor, raised in a white-collar home and related to an executive whose job is to cut costs to preserve a company, was more sympathetic to the corporation. Working together, these pastors provided a balanced pastoral approach to the situation. However, this became possible only after they named their operating assumptions and acknowledged them as biases.

Finally, preachers should consider how congruent their biases, opinions, and emotions are with those of their listeners. Are the preacher and the congregation on the same page or at opposite ends of the spectrum? This relationship shapes the content, form, and delivery of the transitional sermon. When pastor and congregation are in agreement, the sermon can move directly to their mutual concerns and harness their shared energy. When pastor and congregation are in disagreement, the sermon needs to demonstrate the preacher's comprehension of the congregation's position, overcome the listeners' emotional and intellectual defenses, and interest and engage the congregation in considering another perspective. When the congregation does not understand the change and transition or does not hold a particular position, the preacher must provide both information and a method to help congregants comprehend and respond. Regardless of the circumstance, pastors experienced in preaching through transitions advise, "Be honest. Steady as she goes. Do what is *true,* even when it may not be what is *right.*"

Understanding the journey of transition, trusting the act of preaching to be an effective partner in leading the congregation, preparing the transitional sermon, and engaging in holy and active listening are difficult and demanding tasks. They are made more complicated and challenging by the uncertainty and upheaval that change and transition bring to the lives of everyone they touch, whether individually or corporately. To fulfill these commitments faithfully and responsibly, preachers need to be centered in God and grounded in their faith. In the next chapter, I explore how, in the midst of the chaos, confusion, and contradiction of change and transition, the preacher maintains the peace, security, confidence, and perspective that come from being anchored in God.

Questions for Reflection

- Name your greatest strength and your greatest weakness as a listener.
- What mechanisms do you use to listen to your congregation?
- Describe your congregation's health, culture, and norms for dealing with conflict.
- Do you understand part of your role as pastor to be serving as an agent of change? Why or why not?
- Name three assumptions that might bias the way you preach through a congregational transition.

CHAPTER 5

ANCHORED IN GOD

Toward the end of the pastoral consultation that undergirds this book, one participant expressed what was obviously a deeply felt concern: "We haven't talked about how hard leading a congregation through transition is. It can be debilitating. It can be lonely. There's little support." As the group's leader, I responded that, throughout our time together, I had heard loud and clear from the consultants how difficult preaching and leading are in times of congregational transition. Some of that conversation took place in small groups and outside programmed activities, often on the edges and beneath the surface of other conversations. As the consultants and I talked, it became clear that addressing this concern indirectly is precisely the problem. Frequently, the physical exhaustion, isolation, emotional depletion, and spiritual imbalance that preachers regularly experience during congregational transitions get pushed to the edges of pastoral ministry and buried beneath the surface of other conversations and concerns. One pastor commented, "It is easy to set aside feelings during the transition, and then they come back later. We clergy tend not to think about how we are doing. We set aside our own stuff and become high-functioning, unfeeling automatons." Other pastors agreed: "During congregational transitions, pastors often function rather than feel. We lose track of how we are feeling in the transition—hurt, unaffected, bored, fragile, vulnerable, under attack. But feelings will catch up." Left unaddressed, the preacher's anger, sadness, disappointment, and stress will reveal themselves in preaching.

In this chapter, I will attempt to bring this concern to the forefront. Our purpose, the consultants' and mine, is to sound the alert that it is essential to preaching and leading that preachers remain centered in themselves and anchored in God amid the storms of congregational transition. It is also difficult to do so. When preachers are centered, they distinguish between their lives and the lives of the congregation and transition, and they differentiate between themselves and their role. When preachers are anchored in God, the congregation, an agenda, and results do not exercise ultimate authority in the preacher's life and ministry. Though the congregation, agenda, and results influence preachers, God is both the source of life and the final authority who empowers, directs, and evaluates their ministry. Empowered by God, preachers dare to be faithful, even when risking in faith means falling into traps, making mistakes, and needing to refocus when ministry gets distorted. Anchored in God, preachers will not allow the congregation, transition, or results to become their "golden calf" (Exod. 32:1-20).

If you are feeling either well grounded or eager to listen to and learn more about your congregation's transition as you continue the sermon preparation process, you may want to turn to the second part of this book and consult the relevant "transition brief," returning to this chapter as needed. The pastors consulted in preparing this book are clear that remaining centered and anchored in God is tough work because, at the very least, the congregation, the transition, and the preacher's own sense of identity and self-worth vie for our attention and energy. Preachers therefore need to attend to their relationships with themselves and with God. In considering how preachers might do this, I do not offer a how-to manual or self-help guide. Instead, I first suggest issues of which preachers should be aware, issues that have the potential to threaten well-being. I will then explore the gift of being anchored in God. Finally, I offer avenues that other pastors have found helpful in maintaining their well-being—practices that preachers feeling tossed and turned by transition might choose to investigate.

ISSUES TO BE AWARE OF

During congregational transitions, every preacher is fragile—at different points, in different ways, and to different degrees. The need for clergy to care for themselves transcends individuals and faith traditions. Experiencing exhaustion, imbalance, doubt, and depletion is not in itself an indication of failure, weakness, or unfaithfulness. Rather, these are the inevitable consequences of leading a congregational transition and attempting to preach through it—inherently dangerous work.

In *Leadership on the Line: Staying Alive Through the Dangers of Leading*, Ronald Heifetz and Marty Linsky of Harvard University's John F. Kennedy School of Government observe: "The dangers of exercising leadership derive from the nature of the problems for which leadership is necessary. Adaptive change stimulates resistance because it challenges people's habits, beliefs, and values."[1] Leading a congregation through transition involves what Heifetz and Linsky call "adaptive change." In congregational transitions, we ask people to face "a whole host of problems that are not amenable to authoritative expertise or standard operating procedures. . . . They require experiments, new discoveries, and adjustments from numerous places in the organization and community. Without learning new ways—changing attitudes, values and behaviors—people cannot make the adaptive leap necessary to thrive in the new environment."[2] As I said, making this leap requires that people experience loss, embrace uncertainty, and turn their backs on cherished identity and ways of doing and being. Heifetz and Linsky continue, "Because adaptive change forces people to question and perhaps redefine aspects of their identity, it also challenges their sense of competence. Loss, disloyalty, and feeling incompetent: That's a lot to ask. No wonder people resist."[3]

In chapter 1 I discussed the reasons people resist change. Here I highlight the intensity and direction of the congregation's resistance. Pastors in congregational transitions soon discover that people's capacities to deny, forget, and resist are strong. People work hard to stay in control and to do things as they always have. People will fight to hold on to assumptions, attitudes, and activities they hold dear, particularly those that had a positive effect on the congregation's life and ministry in the past. At its best, resistance is an indication that the congregation cares deeply about the church and community and is a sign of health in that the change and transition have not shocked or depressed the congregation into complacency. The negative aspects of the congregation's history also influence the intensity and direction of resistance. When old wounds open and old memories surface, the pastor might become the focus of people's feelings about God, another pastor, or issues in the pastoral relationship. Stated simply, the congregation's resistance is often directed squarely at the pastor. Reflecting on this experience, a pastor sighed, "Hurting people will hurt you, and broken people will break you."

As I said, denial is often the congregation's preferred means of resistance. People will deny the problems that necessitate change, particularly if those problems are related in some way to either their own prejudice or injustice within the congregation. People's capacity to deny problems greatly increases when admitting a problem reveals that they hold biases and act in ways that contradict their faith. Even when pastors understand and successfully address the reasons people resist, the congregation's perceptions and reactions rarely remain stable over time. Pastors might find themselves repeatedly listening and responding to the same people who have new and different concerns.

Congregations also resist for no discernable reason. As I said in chapter 1, Charles Campbell argues that some forms of resistance are not easily comprehended and overcome because, rather than the result of misunderstanding and loss, they are the work of forces determined to silence and divide the congregation and to undermine, sidetrack, and derail the transition. These forces often manifest themselves in parishioners who, for inexplicable reasons, resist for the sake of resisting, to the point that they personally attack the pastor. In so doing, these people often become what one consultant labeled "lightening rods for the pastor, people that spark all sorts of emotions." Over time, congregational resistance becomes tedious, distracting, and exhausting. Since resistance is so strong and pervasive, pastors need to find ways of coping so that they are not completely surprised, overwhelmed, or defeated by the intensity, manifestations, and resilience of the congregation's resistance to the transition.

Coping with resistance would be difficult enough if leaders had a well-developed plan, confidence that what they are doing is right, and sufficient time to prepare, reflect, and wait for the congregation to respond positively. Unfortunately, these are luxuries that congregations and transitions rarely afford their leaders. For many pastors and congregations, the change brings a sense of urgency, and the transition is unfamiliar territory. Panic is the frequent companion of both pastors and congregants. Experiencing both internal and external pressure to come up with a response, a direction, or a plan, leaders often do not make the best use of the limited time they have. Either they spend their time inefficiently or they waste time fretting over how little time they have. Losing valuable time often intensifies leaders' sense of urgency. Once the response, direction, or plan is determined, the challenge becomes staying focused. Heifetz and Linsky warn, "There are many ways in which communities and organizations will consciously or subconsciously try to make you lose focus. They do this sometimes by broadening your agenda, sometimes by overwhelming it, but always with a seemingly logical reason for disruption."[4]

Another reason that congregational transitions are personally difficult for those who lead them is that pastors and parishioners frequently find themselves in different places on the journey of transition. This difference results in part because pastors commonly receive information earlier or in greater detail than the congregation does. This difference also occurs because pastors spend more time thinking about and are more directly affected by the transition. That a pastor and a congregation are in different places in a transition is most obvious in a pastoral transition. By the time the congregation is informed of the change, the pastor has already decided to leave and begun the process of ending ministry.

Preachers easily become distracted and experience themselves as adrift when, as I indicated in chapter 1, the congregational transition creates a personal transition in the life of the preacher. For example, in pastoral transitions, departing pastors must attend to personal feelings such as grief, relief, excitement, and guilt over what the congregation is experiencing at the same time they are attending to the congregation's feelings of betrayal, anger, and loss. Or, pastors may resolve their own feelings, make an ending or new beginning, and find themselves impatiently waiting for the congregation to catch up.

Yet another reason that remaining centered and anchored is difficult is that congregational transitions often lack resolution, both in themselves and in the heart and the life of the preacher. Most often, what the preacher and congregation hope will happen does not turn out exactly as they expect. In fact, their vision may never see life. A pastor complained, "It is hard to give your energy when you sense no change will really occur." Disappointment, regret, and second-guessing might blossom into feelings of incompetence and failure, even long after the transition. Years after leading a congregation to complete its ministry, a pastor reported that, when she thinks back to those days, she still worries that she made the wrong decision and failed her congregation. Asked what she would have done if the congregation had decided not to close, the pastor responded, "Probably still be there."

Like congregational transitions themselves, preaching in times of congregational transition can also undermine and challenge the preacher. Even at its best, whenever preaching brings people face-to-face with what they would rather deny, consequences will follow for the preacher. Naming a change and addressing a transition from the pulpit may introduce or escalate a sense of crisis in the congregation. The pastor may be blamed for creating the problem and upsetting the congregation. Worse, the congregation may decide that the pastor is the problem; the pastor is the reason that people are upset. Heifetz and Linsky observe: "Generally, people do not authorize someone to make them face what they do not want to face. Instead people hire someone to provide protection and ensure stability, someone with solutions that require a minimum of disruption."[5] Pastors who seriously embrace the role of change agent may become the lightening rod that attracts all of the congregation's fear, anger, anxiety, and doubt.

Preaching through transition is also difficult for preachers because, while they can often concretely and specifically name what the congregation must end and give up, they cannot guarantee results. The most they can guarantee is God's presence and love. Beyond this, preachers can offer only a vision and a hope. Heifetz and Linsky describe this reality saying, "when you lead people through change, you challenge what people hold dear—their daily habits, tools, loyalties, and ways of thinking—with nothing more to offer perhaps than a possibility."[6] When the possibility does not materialize exactly or as quickly as the people heard in transitional sermons or expected for reasons of their own, the preacher may become the congregation's scapegoat.

Biblically speaking, the scapegoat makes atonement for the people by bearing all of their transgressions on its head and then being sent away into the wilderness.[7] The result of preaching through transition may be that many sins are laid on the preacher's head. The pastor may be blamed for the change and for the congregation's experience of loss, including the loss of permanence and stability. Like Moses, the preacher may also be blamed for the difficulty and disorientation of the transition.[8] The pastor's leadership will surely be questioned, even maligned. The pastor may be accused of being uncaring. Recalling that in many congregations change is not possible until everyone is on board, the pastor may be criticized both because members of the congregation are unhappy and because the pastor is perceived to be making the change before everyone has agreed to it or is comfortable with it. The pastor may be accused of dividing the congregation and making worship an unsafe place. Those who disagree with the need for or reality of change, the direction the transition is taking, or the pastor will accuse the pastor of disregarding or disrespecting the past, the way things were, the way the congregation has always done things, and longtime members.

Once they become the repository of the congregation's sin, preachers, like the biblical scapegoat, may find themselves banished to the wilderness. Heifetz and Linsky warn, "Asking people to leave behind something they have lived with for years or for generations practically invites them to get rid of you. Sometimes leaders are taken out simply because they do not appreciate the sacrifice they are asking from others."[9] The pastor and the pastor's family may become isolated. On occasion, preachers lose their positions, bringing the accompanying losses of livelihood and reputation. Less tangibly, congregational transitions may cost the pastor the congregation's trust, even trust developed over many years. When a shortage of Roman Catholic clergy required that a congregation make a transition from a pastoral staff to a single priest, people distrusted the motives of both the diocesan bishop and the priests when they changed the number and schedule of worship services and reorganized and delegated responsibilities within the parish. In response to what the clergy considered prayerful and deliberate decisions to do what was best for the congregation, people wrote accusatory letters, attempted to triangulate the priests, and mounted a communal effort to petition the bishop.

For all these reasons, some pastors report that they are afraid of staying in a church in transition too long. They fear being irreparably drained of their energy and passion, and personally damaged. Pastors also fear being inappropriately labeled by their colleagues and representatives of the greater church. For example, after leading a congregation to complete its ministry, I was unnerved to attend a pastors' meeting and discover that, among some clergy, I was labeled a "closer" who "failed" as opposed to a "missionary" or "evangelist." Despite the reality of these fears, pastors who succeed at preaching and leading congregations through transition agree that the key to not losing themselves in the process is intentionally doing things that promote a strong sense of self and an even stronger reliance on God.

THE GIFT OF BEING ANCHORED IN GOD

As simple as it sounds and as difficult as it is, the key to remaining centered in ourselves is being anchored in God. Writing these words, I am struck by how obvious a statement this is. In times of congregational transition, as in every season of ministry, preachers need to do all they can to actively rely upon God. The problem, of course, is that we simply do not do this. We are so occupied with and even overwhelmed by all that we have to do that self-care begins to feel like a distraction. Even though we know that we need to attend to ourselves and to God, we just can't find the time. Or, we are handling things so successfully that we assume both our ability to cope and our relationship with God are in good shape. Either way, we are so busy relying on ourselves to do for God that we neglect to rely upon God to do for us and our congregations.

Rather than suggesting anything revolutionary, perhaps the most beneficial thing I can do is to remind preachers that relying on God anchors us in at least five ways. First, when we rely on God rather than on ourselves or anything else, we trust Paul's words that, regardless of what we do or fail to do, nothing will be able to separate us from God's love (Rom. 8.39). At its best, this assurance frees preachers to risk, to try, and to fail as we strive faithfully to preach to and lead God's people. At its best, this assurance also empowers preachers to speak the truth in love. At the same time, our own fears, doubts, and insecurities, together with the realities of life, both in the church and in the world, make trusting this promise an ongoing struggle. As one pastor commented, "I know that eternity will turn out all right. I'm not so sure about the congregational meeting."

Second, when we rely on God, we understand that, ultimately, we are not alone. Belonging to God means that we also belong to God's people. Scripture repeatedly declares that we are a people holy to God; that God has chosen us to be God's people, God's treasured possession (Deut. 7:6).[10] We belong to a community that transcends congregation, circumstance, change, and transition. This community does not depend upon us, on whether people agree and get along, on whether we do the right thing, or whether we do anything at all. This community depends upon and is held together by God. Tangible expressions of this community—including relationships between individuals and groups, our ministry with a congregation, and even a congregation's life—may end. Nevertheless, the life of God's people continues. Of course, our attachment to tangible expressions of God's people is very strong; as manifestations of God's people, tangible expressions need to be protected, cherished, and nourished. At the same time, relying on God helps both preachers and congregations not to confuse maintaining the congregation with participating in the continuing life of God's people.

Third, placing our ministry in the context of God's ongoing work of redemption provides a profound sense of meaning and purpose that transcends individuals, congregations, and circumstances. While God is deeply concerned with us, our ministries, our congregations, and their transitions, God's purpose is bigger. Luke describes God's purpose as bringing good news to the poor, proclaiming release to the captives and recovery of sight to the blind, freeing the oppressed, and proclaiming the year of the Lord's favor (Luke 4:18-19). In chapter 3, I described God as doing new things and acting in new ways to love, save, and renew. Paul tells us that God's purpose is bigger than our congregations; "the creation itself will be set free from its bondage to decay and will obtain the freedom of the glory of the children of God" (Rom. 8:21). Too often we become so focused on our work, our congregation, and its transition that we fail to take in the panoramic view and grasp the grandeur of God's purpose and design. The "cloud of witnesses" that surrounds us reminds us that God's purpose preceded these circumstances and our efforts and will continue long after they have passed. Trusting that our preaching and ministry are part of God's greater work, we can dare to lay aside every weight that clings to us and run with perseverance the race that is set before us (Heb. 12:1).

Fourth, God's Word will guide us and God's promises sustain us. I intend this statement more as a prayer than a prediction. When I say that God's Word will guide us, I do not mean that we can open the Bible and find an exact blueprint for our transition. Sometimes, Moses' words to Israel are the closest thing to a plan that we find: "I call heaven and earth to witness against you today that I have set before you life and death, blessings and curses. Choose life so that you and your descendants may live" (Deut. 30:19). But what does it mean to choose life? Nor can we presume that God will support us in the ways that we would choose or think best. As I have said repeatedly, actively engaging the breadth of Scripture provides greater understanding of and response to the congregation and its transition. Receiving God's promises and engaging God in prayer lead us to incorporate

God's promises into our circumstances. Time and again pastors leading congregational transitions describe themselves as Jacob. After a long night of wrestling with God, they come away both wounded and blessed (Gen. 14:24-32). Praying rather than predicting, we experience that God's Word is a lamp to our feet and a light to our path (Psalm 119:105). Rather than finding answers, we know that "truly God has listened; God has given heed to the words of my prayer" (Psalm 66:19).

Fifth, relying on God improves preachers' attitude. Preachers can be steadfast, immovable, always excelling in the work of the Lord, because we know that "in the Lord our labor is not in vain" (1 Cor. 15:58). This attitude leads preachers to claim spiritual gifts that empower them to preach and lead through transition. These gifts might be summarized as call, commitment, choice, control, and change. Preachers can claim that their preaching is in response to a specific *call* from God to preach to and lead this congregation—particular people in specific circumstances—through change and transition. For God calls women and men to bring God's word to and guide God's people through the circumstances of life today as surely as God called the prophets, apostles, saints, reformers of the church, and renewers of society who have gone before us.

Preachers who understand themselves as called by God to a particular task have reported experiencing an increased *commitment* to carry out their ministry. They report feeling renewed both to devote the time and energy that ministry demands, and to muster the patience, trust, fortitude, and hope necessary to serve faithfully. Preachers who believe themselves called by God report that they are less afraid of failure and less defeated by denial and resistance. They stay better focused and are less distracted by attacks, even personal attacks. Most important perhaps, preachers better resist the temptation to become victims by recognizing that they always have *choices*. Though choices may not be easy or without consequence, choices exist nonetheless. The recognition of choice prevents preachers from becoming or feeling trapped, silenced, or powerless. When they are free to choose, preachers are better able to identify what they are responsible for and can *control*. Pastors often expend much of their time, energy, and influence on matters in which they lack expertise and do not exercise authority. When pastors understand that their chief responsibilities are to preach, lead worship, care for the poor, and reconcile the estranged, they are less likely to endeavor to undertake the congregation's entire ministry. Instead, preachers will empower others and find themselves more focused. This is possible only when preachers accept *change* as inevitable. Understanding change as neither good nor bad, they strive to embrace change as an opportunity rather than a threat.

Anchored in God and centered in ourselves, we rely upon God above all else, including ourselves, the congregation, results, and a plan for leading the transition because, ultimately, God gives meaning to our lives and validates our ministry. The theological or faith foundation of our reliance on God varies across faith traditions. For some it is baptism; for others it is a covenant. For still others, reliance on God grows from acceptance of a personal relationship with God or Christ. Regardless of how we understand and articulate our reliance on God, discovering and maintaining ways of returning to this foundational relationship on a regular if not daily basis are essential to preaching, leading, and living in times of congregational transition.

AVENUES TO INVESTIGATE

Colleagues in ministry offer several avenues they have found helpful, ways that preachers seeking to center and anchor themselves in God might consider investigating. Just as congregations resist change and transition, so many pastors resist caring for themselves and their relationship with God. This resistance is understandable for at least three reasons. First, the uniqueness of preachers, congregations, and transitions means that, as in congregational transitions generally, no formula is available to follow. One consultant commented, "Lots of stuff in a transition just needs to be figured out. People and contexts differ, and no one can write a recipe for survival."

Second, the demands of ministry lead many pastors to conclude that caring for ourselves and attending to our relationship with God are at best a luxury and at worst signs of selfishness, weakness, or incompetence. We tend to forget that remaining centered ourselves and anchored in God are acts of faithfulness, strength, and mature leadership. We seek balance, refreshment, health, and wholeness so that we can better serve the people and ministry to which God calls us. As one pastor declared, "I am convinced that preachers need to find ways to keep themselves healthy if they are going to lead congregations through transition in beneficial ways."

Third, since caring for ourselves and attending to our relationship with God is an open-ended process that changes with time and circumstance, it is the aspect of preaching and leading through congregational transition that many preachers, including this one, struggle with most. Just when we think we have a handle on how to do it, something changes, and we find ourselves heading back to the drawing board.

These days, as I return to the drawing board, I ask pastors who lead congregations through transition how they remain grounded and connected to God. Since I am someone who struggles with remaining grounded and connected to God in times of change, part of my interest is selfish. At some level I hope to uncover something akin to a program, plan, or formula that makes maintaining a serene and stable inner life and a potent and palpable connection to God easy and lasting. I am repeatedly gratified to hear that, like me, pastors whom I respect also continue to struggle to remain grounded and connected to God. They affirm that monitoring ourselves and seeking guidance from others are themselves ways of centering and anchoring. Seasoned pastors confirm that there is no magic wand to wave, no formula to follow. They are also eager to share practices that they have found helpful. Reflecting on these conversations, I can identify 10 avenues that pastors might investigate while seeking to steady the ship of their lives and ministries while sailing the often turbulent seas of congregational transition.

First, *preaching* in times of congregational transition can be a public act of ministry for the preacher as well as for the congregation. A consultant observed, "The African American preacher often finds that preaching in times of transition can be powerful and spirit-filled. The preacher often finds himself or herself drenched with the Spirit and filled with God's presence. It is a blessing that nurtures the preacher in the midst of transition." Several consultants recalled advice that John Wesley received: "Preach faith till you have it; and then, because you have it, you will preach faith."[11] Their point is that preaching not only ministers to others; it also ministers to the preacher. When preachers listen to their own sermons, when they allow themselves to hear the claim made upon them but especially the promise made to them, the message has the power to disclose new ways of being and living for preachers as well as for their hearers. A preacher listens to her or his own sermons by becoming the first and perhaps principal hearer of everything in the sermon. As preachers reflect on, write, practice, and preach their sermons, they respond appropriately to what they hear before they expect any response from their congregations.

When preachers cannot hear God speak in their own preaching, they worship in other faith communities where they can hear the gospel from another preacher. When asked how to worship elsewhere, pastors suggested attending midweek worship services in neighboring congregations, on college and university campuses, or at institutions such as hospitals and nursing homes. Pastors said it is important to choose faith communities where they know they will be welcome and where they will hear a word from the Lord. These colleagues emphasize that they attend these services to worship, not to lead. Some arrive just after the service starts and leave just before it is over to remind themselves and others that they are not there in any official capacity and to avoid questions and conversations about congregation and church. They do whatever it takes to hear God's love and promises proclaimed to them. "Be preached to!" The rabbi in our group insisted, "If you can't find a Christian church, go to temple!," assuring us that we would be most welcome.

A second way that preachers stay immersed in God's word is by undertaking *Bible study* strictly for themselves. In our work of preaching, teaching, pastoral care, and leading, we often study Scripture for others. When we read or listen to Scripture to hear God addressing us personally, God returns us to Godself. God helps us to experience our lives and ministries as connected to the divine work of salvation. "Speak, Lord, for your servant is listening" (1 Sam. 3:9) is our hermeneutic key to these Bible studies. When I consult with pastors, I increasingly ask them to name a biblical image or story that reflects their life journey. For example, at the conclusion of my first year in my current teaching position, my wife and I were weighing the pros and cons of remaining in this place. When we became less pragmatic, laid aside our lists, and listened for a word from God, we found ourselves captivated by God's command to Abram: "Now the Lord said to Abram, 'Go from your country and your kindred and your father's house to the land that I will show you.'" (Gen. 12:1). While Cathy and I were not excessively concerned about becoming great, and had no desire to become a nation, we suddenly understood ourselves to be on a journey from home in response to God's command, unsure of the new land that the Lord was showing us and hoping both to be a blessing and to be blessed. Four years later, we are mindful of Moses' words to Israel: "See, the Lord your God has given the land to you; go up, take possession, as the Lord, the God of your ancestors, has promised you; do not fear or be dismayed" (Deut. 1:21). Convinced that God through the church has called us to this

place, this ministry, and this community, we are about the work of mutually possessing and being possessed by God's people and our shared mission and ministry in this place. By paying attention to how Scripture
addressed us personally, Cathy and I came to an understanding of God's
calling for us.

I recently heard Frank Thomas, pastor of Mississippi Boulevard Christian Church in Memphis, echo Deuteronomy in reminding preachers that
bringing Scripture to bear on our own lives

> is not too hard for you, nor is it too far away. [God's word] is not in
> heaven, that you should say, "Who will go up to heaven for us, and get it
> for us so that we may hear it and observe it?" Neither is it beyond the
> sea, that you should say, "Who will cross to the other side of the sea for
> us, and get it for us so that we may hear it and observe it?" No, the word
> is very near to you; it is in your mouth and in your heart for you to
> observe.
>
> —Deuteronomy 30:11-14

Sometimes God's word is silenced and stopped by the work of congregational transition. God's word nevertheless remains within us. When we study
Scripture for ourselves, God opens our mouths and touches our hearts to
awaken in us what we already know.

Third, in response to God's word, we *pray*. Fred Craddock reminds
preachers that "the minister is prepared by the study and reflection that
has gone into the sermon and by the prayer in which the sermon has been
bathed."[12] Pastors leading congregational transitions recount points along
the journey when prayer was the only way they managed to get either themselves or their people through. Pastors report that they pray for inner peace
and the grace to be calm and focused. They pray for confidence in God's
ability to make their congregations open to receive God's word and to respond in faith. Pastors pray for themselves, for other leaders, and for their
families. Some pastors include prayers for themselves in the petitions during worship. Pastors report that during congregational transitions, much
of their prayer is about reminding God and themselves of who God is and
what God has promised. Many pastors describe their prayer during congregational transitions as a daylong conversation with God. Resonating
with Paul's command to "pray without ceasing" (1 Thess. 5:17), these pastors pray "on the go" as they move from place to place and from task to

task. They make it a point to pray with the people they encounter. Other pastors report that in the fast pace of transition, they follow Jesus' example and withdraw to a deserted place apart to pray (Mark 1:35). There they sit still and silent before God. Still others recruit others to pray for and with them. Whatever pattern we select, *how* we pray is less important than *that* we pray.

Fourth, hearing God's word and encountering God in prayer leads us to praise God in *worship*. Earlier, I talked about preachers' need to hear God's word preached to them. Preachers also need to respond to God, to worship God for themselves and for their lives. Preachers report that, particularly during transitions in their congregations, they are eager for opportunities to worship. Pastors from sacramental traditions share how important the Lord's Supper, baptismal remembrance, and confession and absolution are to them. These rites provide opportunities for the preacher to receive God's grace and for the congregation to experience God's love in ways that, unlike preaching, do not directly depend upon the minister. A pastor reflected, "In Holy Communion, I know that my people and I will receive God's grace. I can't always say that about my preaching." Preachers also greatly appreciate sharing worship leadership with other leaders and the congregation. Congregational hymns, choir anthems and special music, listening as a member of the congregation reads Scripture, and hearing the people of God pray become particularly meaningful. At its best, the congregation's worship provides respite for the preacher because the people are united as the congregation takes refuge in the shadow of God's wings.[13] When the congregation's worship does not provide an experience of God's grace, many preachers seek other opportunities to sing, pray, and worship with God's people.

Fifth, preaching requires balance. Balance calls us to a time of rest or *sabbath*. During sabbath rest, we give attention to our physical, interpersonal, vocational, intellectual, emotional, and spiritual selves. To maintain balance, preachers carve out time to achieve distance and perspective on a vocation that is emotionally demanding. We establish a rhythm of pausing to pay attention to ordinary life. We make time to take things in, to uncover what lies deeply within us, and to mull things over. We also cultivate our ability to step back. We call a halt to expending energy frantically. We joyously offer the gifts of our undivided attention and our presence to our own lives and to those we love. Biblically speaking, preachers "remember the sabbath day, and keep it holy" (Exod. 20:8). In obedience to God's command, we name, claim, and keep a specific day (or equivalent period) of rest.

It is easier to keep sabbath when preachers have a life beyond their ministry, the congregation, and the transition and when they do not take that life for granted. Preachers cherish relationships with family; single preachers honor and protect significant relationships as their family. Preachers also cultivate relationships outside their congregations. They pursue interests beyond their ministry. An economist once suggested to me that the key to a healthy life is diversification, not putting all of our life's eggs in one basket. When we do not have a life beyond our ministry and congregation, our lives get reduced to our role. Heifetz and Linksy warn, "Confusing role with self is a trap. Even though you may put all of yourself into your role—your passions, values, and artistry—the people in your setting will be reacting to you, not primarily as a person, but as the role you take in their lives."[14] These authors suggest that having a life beyond our roles may enable us to bear furious opposition, even from our own friends and former collaborators, who remake our role overnight from darling to outcast. When we have a life beyond our roles, we may find the stamina to remain gentle, focused, and persistent.[15] Heifetz and Linsky suggest that, more than enabling us to resist opposition, "knowing and valuing yourself, distinct from the roles you play, you gain the freedom to take risks within those roles. Your self-worth is not so tightly tied to the reactions of other people as they contend with your positions on issues."[16]

Asked how to cultivate a life beyond the congregation, many pastors spoke of the importance of their families. These pastors invest heavily in familial relationships, making their home life, regular family outings, and participation in their spouse's and children's activities top priorities. As one pastor remarked, "I can handle the transition because I'm OK at home." Others spoke of maintaining friendships outside the congregation, the faith tradition, and even the church. Still others emphasized activities that do more than take them away from work; these pastors urge doing things that actively nurture other dimensions of their well-being.

Keeping sabbath is also easier when preachers establish practices that distance them from their work. Heifetz and Linsky correctly point out that, to prevent their professional selves from seeping into their personal lives, both women and men need rituals to help peel away their professional roles so they can feel their own skins again.[17] Ministry requires personal integration, and we should be uncomfortable when there is a great dichotomy between our pastoral and personal selves. But we should be equally uncomfortable when our personal and pastoral selves become indistinguishable. We all need times and places when we take the clerical collar off; we all need people for whom we will never be the pastor. Pastors therefore need to develop rituals for crossing the threshold between their public ministry and their personal lives. Almost any simple act will do. Some pastors clear their desks before they leave the office; others use the trip home to clear their minds. I wear a suit or coat and tie when I am working and more casual attire ("play clothes") when I am not. A pastor who works out of the house leaves his home study every evening and goes out for a cup of coffee so that he can return home. Any activity can be turned into a ritual and combined with intentional awareness that one is leaving work behind.

At times in the common life of a pastor and congregation, the best way to guarantee that the pastor finds a sabbath rest is to suggest, or even mandate, that the congregation take sabbath time as well. In one congregation, when the members of the congregational council and even the pastor shared with one another that they resented coming to church because Sunday had become an extended business meeting, the congregation determined to "remember the sabbath day, and keep it holy" by decreeing that church business will not be conducted on Sunday. The church gathered on Sunday for worship, fellowship, Bible study, and prayer. However, meetings, decisions, and even conversations about the congregation's life and future were relegated to the rest of the week. By efficiently using telephone and e-mail, the leaders were able to reclaim Sunday as a day of rest and refreshment without increasing their commitments during the week.

In a congregation that spent two years claiming a new vision for mission and undertaking a successful capital campaign, the pastor knew that he was exhausted but did not know how to slow down. As I listened, I was impressed by all that the pastor and congregation had accomplished. I asked if they had taken time to celebrate. I wondered if, like God, they had paused to see everything that they had made, that indeed, it was very good.[18] I mused about the possibility of the congregation's declaring a kind of jubilee, a week of Sundays or seven weeks in which the congregation would celebrate the work it had done together and confine its efforts to the foundational ministries of congregational life, including worship, prayer, care, fellowship, reflection, and keeping sabbath. Strictly speaking, a jubilee is the final year in a cycle of 50 years. Jubilee was originally a time of emancipation and the return of property to its original owner; however, I was attracted to the Jubilee's spirit of liberty and restoration in a broader sense. The pastor and the congregation needed to be set free to see all they had accomplished rather than feeling bound to everything that they still have to do. As we talked, a seven-week sermon series emerged. The themes for the weeks:

1. "Guilt for Resting: How Can We Do This?"
2. "Fear: Will It All Fall Apart While We Do Nothing?"
3. "Recognition: I'm Resting!"
4. "The Gift of Rest"
5. "Opening Ourselves to Listen to God During the Sabbath"
6. "Share What We are Hearing and Learning"
7. "Wake Up and Celebrate! It's Time to Get Back Out There!"

Using these themes, the driven pastor and the busy congregation dedicated the seven weeks before their September startup to keeping sabbath.

Sixth, pastors who remained healthy during significant congregational transitions said that it is essential that preachers *maintain spiritual disciplines*. Traditionally understood, keeping the sabbath, worship, prayer, use of the sacraments, Bible study, and confession and forgiveness are considered spiritual disciplines. Other spiritual disciplines include simplicity, fasting, keeping silence, acts of charity, tithing, and meeting with a spiritual director. Pastors emphasize that *maintaining* is distinct from *undertaking* spiritual disciplines. Their point is that the onset of a significant congregational transition is not the ideal time to begin attending to our spiritual lives. While we may need to do this if we have neglected our spiritual lives, establishing spiritual disciplines that we can rely upon before a change and transition within the congregation is a far better practice. Colleagues were also clear that preachers should be more concerned with using disciplines that work for them than with doing what is expected. For example, I am a "night owl," not an "early bird." Despite my best intentions, I am simply not awake enough to "sing aloud of [God's] steadfast love in the morning" (Psalm 59:16). My spiritual life was greatly enhanced when I gave up the expectation of early-morning devotions. Instead, I prefer a time of listening to Scripture, silence, and prayer before bed.

The remaining four practices that colleagues identified as important ways of staying centered and anchored in God might be approached as less traditional spiritual disciplines. They are:

- guarding your heart,
- seeking sanctuary,
- managing stress, and
- having mentors.

To remain centered and anchored during congregational transitions, leaders need to develop a thick skin and not take things personally. Heifetz and Linsky declare:

> Leadership takes the capacity to stomach hostility so that you can stay connected to people, lest you disengage from them and exacerbate the danger. They warn, "Raising questions that go to the core of people's habits goes unrewarded, at least for a while. You get booed instead of cheered. In fact, it may be a long time before you hear any applause—if ever. They may throw tomatoes. They may shoot bullets."[19]

One consultant warned, "It's not enough to brace yourself for not being appreciated; you need to *guard your heart* so that it doesn't get broken." We guard our hearts when we resist taking everything personally. We guard our hearts by refusing to view ourselves as the cause of and the reason for whatever is happening in the congregation. Instead we sift through whatever is happening to separate the things for which we are responsible from the things others are responsible for, the consequences of the transition, and the feelings that people are attempting to attach to us, whether personally or to the pastoral office that we hold. We also guard our hearts by finding people outside the congregation with whom it is appropriate and safe to express heartache and heartbreak and regularly taking the opportunity to do so.

Eighth, preachers also guard their hearts when they *seek sanctuary*. Heifetz and Linsky define *sanctuary* as "a place of reflection and renewal, where you can listen to yourself away from the dance floor and the blare of the music, where you can reaffirm your deeper sense of self and purpose."[20] A sanctuary is removed from the world of the congregation; it is a place where you feel physically and psychologically safe. A sanctuary is a place where the rules and stresses of everyday life are temporarily suspended. It is a haven, not a hideout. Having a readily available sanctuary provides a physical anchor and source of sustenance, a place to restore, reflect, and regroup. These days, my sanctuaries include a daily walk to Lake Michigan, the study where I write, regular trips to a favorite restaurant in downtown Chicago, and three weeks away from everything related to work each year. Other pastors I know run marathons, cook, dance, work with wood, and run their model trains.

Leaders of God's people have always sought sanctuary. For example, Moses and Elijah found sanctuary on a mountain. Jesus repeatedly sought sanctuary from the demands of ministry by withdrawing by himself to a deserted place. Jesus sometimes sought sanctuary on a mountain, in a garden, or in the home of a friend.[21] According to Mark, Jesus said to the disciples, "'Come away to a deserted place all by yourselves and rest a while.' For many were coming and going, and they had no leisure even to eat" (6:31). When we are doing our most difficult work, we need to maintain the structures in our lives that center us and keep us healthy. The problem, of course, is that, under stress and pressed for time, our sources of sanctuary are the first comforts we give up as luxuries we can no longer afford.

Ninth, preachers need a *routine of stress management*, in addition to sanctuary and sabbath. The ways people manage stress are as unique as the people who use them. Some preachers use schedule and routine; they have set times for set tasks and, except for extreme pastoral emergencies, they keep their calendars. Some preachers use physical activity, ranging from sports as rigorous as racquetball to practices as soothing as soaking in a hot tub followed by a massage. For some preachers, stress management is a matter of attitude; they consciously make the effort to see the best in others, express appreciation rather than complain, and look for God working in all that happens each day. For other preachers, stress relief comes from mission clarity; they are clear with themselves and others what their role is and is not. Preachers use prayer, meditation, candles, music, and all sorts of hobbies to relieve their stress. The common element is finding something that completely distracts them from their work, even if that activity is itself challenging.

Tenth and finally, none of us can stay centered and anchored by ourselves; we need the help of others. Heifetz and Linsky observe that "even people with great authority and a powerful vision need partners when they are trying to bring about a deep change in community."[22] In times of congregational transition, clergy need two *mentors*. They need both a pastor and a guide in addition to family and friends. First, clergy need to meet regularly with their own pastor, someone outside the congregation whose sole job is to help the preacher process his or her own reactions and responses. In these sessions, the preacher and nothing else is the focus. Though we call the person with whom the preacher meets a pastor, that person need not be ordained. In order to avoid dual relationships and to make it safer for the preacher to share, the person should not be a member of the preacher's denomination. Therapists, counselors, spiritual directors, and institutional chaplains can be great resources. Regardless of whom preachers choose, they need to find such a person and a way of dealing with the transition for themselves; preachers need regular times when they are themselves the focus.

As a second mentor, preachers should seek out a guide, someone who has already been on the journey the preacher is taking. The guide might be a veteran pastor with a wealth of experience, or a consultant with expertise in dealing with a particular situation. The guide's purpose is to be a conversation partner, a sounding board, and a warning beacon. This role is different from that of experts who provide the pastor and congregation a standard recipe to follow. In addition to providing valuable assistance, the guide reminds the preacher that he or she is not alone; other pastors and congregations have passed this way before.

The avenues that the consultants and I offer here are by no means an exhaustive list. Preachers and leaders dealing with congregational transitions report that their own spiritual lives are marked by endings, liminal strands, and new beginnings. When preachers are conscious of this reality and committed to remaining centered and anchored in God, they discover new and exciting roads by which God returns them to Godself and connects their lives and ministries to the very life and purpose of God.

Trusting that God speaks through change, preachers boldly claim that in times of congregational transition God uses words spoken and heard in the preparation and delivery of sermons to accompany, support, and direct God's people as they move into what is still unknown. As I leave you to consult the relevant "transition brief" in the second part of this volume, or to turn to your keyboard or legal pad and prepare Sunday's sermon, I offer a prayer from the Lutheran liturgy for vespers or evening prayer, which I have come to cherish:

Lord God, you have called your servants to ventures of which we cannot see the ending, by paths as yet untrodden, through perils unknown. Give us faith to go out with good courage, not knowing where we go, but only that your hand is leading us and your love supporting us; through Jesus Christ our Lord.[23]

Questions for Reflection

- How do you feel about yourself, your ministry, your congregation, and the transition?
- Describe your inner world. How would you assess the state of your well-being? How would you assess the state of your relationship with God, both from your perspective and from God's perspective?
- What spiritual disciplines do you find most helpful? How well are you using them? Describe your prayer life. How do you seek sanctuary and hallow the sabbath?
- Who are your pastor and your guide?

TRANSITION BRIEFS

During my doctoral studies at Notre Dame, I learned from James F. White, best known as a pioneer of the liturgical movement, a teacher, and a scholar. I was inspired by Jim's deep concern for the practicalities of Sunday worship, pastoral ministry, and congregational life. Jim's approach to seminar papers reflected this commitment. Rather than assigning the usual 30-page research paper on a single topic, he assigned six-page papers on five separate topics. He reasoned that when busy pastors and professors need to learn something quickly in the midst of their ministries, six pages are about all they have time to read. The task, then, is to write six concise but insightful pages that lay a strong foundation, clearly summarize the issues, provoke reflection and discussion, and suggest further reading. Over the years, many of Jim White's students have found these "White papers" so helpful in our own teaching, pastoral ministry, and research that, with Jim's blessing, we claim this genre as an inheritance.

In the spirit of the "White paper," the second part of this book consists of what I have termed "transition briefs." In this context, I understand a *brief* as a summary of facts, a set of instructions, or information provided in preparation for a task. Though I have permitted myself 10 manuscript pages rather than six, these briefs are brief. They are intended to offer a first word, not the last word. If the preachers we met in the preface called a trusted and experienced colleague, this might be the counsel they would receive. These transition briefs presume familiarity with the first section of this volume. They are written for preachers acquainted with the dynamics of transition, committed to holy and active listening, and prepared to engage preaching as a partner in leading their congregations through transition. In each brief, I attempt to offer counsel on

1. the nature of the transition,
2. voices the preacher should listen for,
3. some biblical stories and images that may prove helpful,
4. sermon preparation in the transition,
5. the struggle to anchor ourselves to God, and
6. a book to read.

Yet these six areas serve more as a springboard than a straitjacket. For each brief, my hope is to prioritize what is most important and helpful.

I offer transition briefs for eight changes that congregations may experience. The most common transition that congregations face occurs from (1) a change of pastor. Some transitions are brought on by changes that are the result of a congregation's normal life cycle, such as (2) a new vision for mission, (3) significant change in the membership or financial giving of the congregation, and (4) completion of the congregation's ministry.

These four changes can be expected as part of the typical congregation's life cycle. William Bridges describes an organization's life cycle as consisting of seven stages.[1] The first stage, *dreaming*, is the time of organization and planning. A congregation works to articulate its vision and to get people to join in bringing that vision into existence. *Launching* the vision, the second life stage, is marked by improvisation rather than by formal systems and policies. In its third life stage, congregations *get organized.* They try to bring order to the chaos by slowing down enough to do things in some organized way. In this life stage, roles become more specialized and more formally defined; experience becomes more important. In its fourth life stage, *making it,* the congregation has what it needs to do significant ministry. Congregations can expand and grow for a very long time in this stage. They begin to reap the rewards of their efforts; the congregation is solidly established and has a basis for continuing expansion. "Making it" leads congregations to feel that they should move from successful to institutional. When a congregation becomes an *institution,* the fifth life stage, its priority shifts from the ministry it accomplishes to the impression it makes. People emphasize what is appropriate for a congregation like this one. In membership and staffing, the concern is less about talent and more about fit. In this life stage, the congregation's reputation is established; pastors and parishioners feel that they have arrived. In its sixth life stage, an institution starts *closing in* on itself and losing vital connections to the outside world, whether that is its immediate neighborhood, the greater church, or contemporary culture. Closing in leads to *dying,* the seventh and final life stage. As a general rule, congregations die in ways that make their pending death less obvious.

Bridges argues that success results in growth and complexity that cannot be contained by the organization's existing form and outlook. Whenever an organization, including a congregation, successfully achieves any stage of organizational development, the accompanying growth and complexity trigger the new stage's demise by creating challenges that stage is not equipped to handle.[2] In an organization's life cycle, transitions are the interludes between one stage of organizational life and the next. Their function is to close out one phase, reorient and renew people in the liminal strand, and begin the next stage. Whenever there is a painful, troubled time in the congregation and the cause is not readily identifiable, a developmental transition is probably occurring. In the first half of the life cycle, not making a transition when the time is ripe for one will cause a "retardation" in the organization that threatens its future development and its very existence. After becoming an institution, a congregation must either choose the path of renewal or choose to die. Renewal, claiming a new vision, means redreaming the dream on which the congregation is based, recapturing the style natural to a young and just-launched congregation, and cultivating a new climate and style of leadership. Transitions from ending one life stage to beginning another life stage can be traumatic because congregations must let go of the very things that got them this far—their sense of identity, ways of doing ministry, and way of living together as a Christian community. People who were most at home in one stage are most likely to experience the next stage as a personal setback.

In addition to the transitions that occur as a natural part of the congregation's life, congregational transitions may result from unanticipated changes. These changes include (5) a traumatic event or tragedy within the congregation, community or nation, (6) a betrayal of trust (financial, sexual, etc.) within the congregation, and (7) an event or issue that creates tension or creates opposition between the church and society. Finally, any change can cause a second congregational transition if (8) factions erupt within the congregation. While other resources provide case studies about congregational life, these briefs take seriously several colleagues' observation that "many readers will be treading water in their own case study—the transition that their congregation is going through." These colleagues implored, "Rather than telling stories, throw them a rope to hold on to!" That is my goal.

CHAPTER 6

PASTORAL TRANSITION

A change in a congregation's pastor creates a transition for the congregation, the pastor who leaves, and the pastor who will come. While the congregation's transition is intertwined and even enmeshed in those of its former and new pastors, the congregation's transition is separate and distinct. This brief presents a pastoral transition from the congregation's perspective.

THE NATURE OF THE TRANSITION

A pastoral transition appears well-defined to a congregation. The *ending* is the conclusion of the departing pastor's ministry. The *liminal strand* is the time when the congregation seeks and calls a new pastor. The *new beginning* is the start of the new pastor's ministry. In reality these divisions are artificial because the transition is fluid; these strands are neither settled nor stable.

During the transition, the congregation experiences at least three preachers—the departing pastor, the arriving pastor, and the interim, judicatory, or guest preacher who fills the pulpit during the vacancy. Preaching during a pastoral transition is therefore an issue not only for the pastor who is leaving and the pastor who is coming. It is also an issue for any pastor who preaches during the interim. Throughout the transition, the congregation and its members need to know that they are loved. Every part of the transition has the potential to reveal shades of betrayal and abandonment—by the pastor(s), the congregation, its leaders, and the church judicatory—and provides an opportunity for factions to fight. Every strand in the transition is also an occasion for the congregation to express and receive gratitude and to cultivate healthy closure.

The *ending* is the time from the pastor's announcing his or her resignation (or new assignment, in appointive systems) to the pastor's leaving the congregation. Pastors announcing their resignation put several dynamics in motion simultaneously. While the congregation is generally caught off guard by the announcement, some congregations and members already know on an intuitive level that their pastor is leaving. A consultant mused, "Does God speak through our members when they ask, 'Are you leaving?' Do they know something we don't? Do they know us better than we know ourselves?"

The congregation—pastor and parishioners alike—experiences grief. While the pastor's emotions are akin to those of someone who is dying, the congregation experiences feelings analogous to emotions felt at the dying of a significant person. People may go through a stage of denial that their pastor will leave. They are angry when they realize that the pastor is leaving and that they were not told in advance. The congregation's anger could be about a lot of things—she won't be here to confirm our kids who adore her; he won't be doing my funeral even though he knows just what I want; we'll have to carry out our new vision all by ourselves. As they seek to make sense of the situation and gain control over it, people may feel guilt, real or imagined, over some burden of personal responsibility for the pastor's departure; they may experience fear about what will happen to their church. Some will experience joy and relief that the pastor is going. The congregation may feel sad over the pastor's departure and feel that it is somehow responsible. The sense of emptiness and loneliness may become heightened if the loss of its pastor causes the congregation to question its ministry and doubt its faithfulness. Some people may become depressed, withdraw, and ultimately leave the congregation. People's expression of grief depends on the nature of their relationship with the pastor. Some might scapegoat each other or the pastor. They may treat the departing pastor as a lame duck. Many in the congregation may want to rush the selection process to secure a new pastor quickly.

The departing, interim, and new pastors all help to ensure that the congregation works through its grief, which can be deep and long lasting. The congregation must resist the temptation to deny or avoid its pain; the pastor needs to resist protecting the congregation from pain. Instead, he or she should give the congregation permission and power to face its grief. When departing pastors fail to let go of their roles in people's lives, and continue to perform pastoral acts for the congregation long after they have ceased to be the pastor, the relationship never ends. When congregations, as total entities, do not experience a "good" termination process, they are carrying their unresolved work with them when both the interim and their next called pastor arrive.[1] During the interim, grief over a former pastor can cause a congregation great difficulty in sound decision making during ministerial selection. When the new pastor arrives, the congregation may be incapable of accepting new pastoral leadership. The new pastor may be forced to listen to stories about the former pastor for a year or longer because the members did not have the opportunity to express their grief directly to the departing pastor. If the departing pastor and congregation are open and vulnerable in their grief, the conclusion of a pastoral ministry provides an opportunity for learning and growth.

The congregation performs four tasks during the *ending* strand. First, leadership assures the congregation that the pastor is not leaving because of anything they did or failed to do. If this is not the case, leaders communicate the reasons for the pastor's departure with candor. Second, the congregation takes control of the situation by developing a plan of action, with an accompanying time line. Third, leaders consult with appropriate people both within and outside the congregation, including church judicatories, to learn the selection process, arrange for worship leadership and preaching, cover pastoral care and visitation, and conduct routine administration. Congregational leaders also work with the departing pastor to ensure that the congregation's ministry continues with minimal interruption. Finally, the congregation creates opportunities for resolution, reconciliation, appreciation, and celebration with the departing pastor that are both meaningful and realistic.

The pastoral vacancy creates a *liminal space.* The vast majority of the congregation manifests a powerful "will to live." One interim pastor likened this will to live to medical caregivers' "getting a pulse" in an emergency room patient. "Once it was clear that their heart was still beating, it seemed simple enough to apply routine pastoral treatment to pull them through." Although they have a will to live, congregations may be reluctant or unable to embrace new life. If some members are ready for resurrection while others desire to tarry at the tomb, the congregation can become deeply divided over the need to move on, resulting in members' finger-pointing over the reasons the congregation seems stalled. The congregation's confidence may be shaken by the departure of its pastor so that the congregation is unable to begin anything new. Often members want to hold off on the resolution of differences "until the new pastor arrives." Some people resist even the basic change represented by the presence of the interim pastor. One interim pastor observed, "Some folks take the opportunity to get while the getting is good, which looks like they wanted to leave anyway but didn't have the wherewithal until the former pastor was gone and the interim arrived. The interim functions as the 'last straw' for these folks."

During a vacancy, the process by which a congregation seeks and selects its pastor is a primary concern. This process is similar to courtship; the selection of a new pastor is not a rational process. Congregations and clergy test each other to see if they like each other and might have a chance at a good future together. No matter how much work the congregation does in terms of self-study, goal-setting, and job description, the decision is most likely to be deeply intuitive, influenced by excitement about the relationship coupled with hope that things will be all right. The most the pastor and congregation can hope for is that they do enough work learning about and getting to know each other before beginning ministry together to cut down on the number of surprises once the relationship begins.

To a greater or lesser degree, the first 12 to 18 months determine a pastor's entire ministry in that congregation.[2] During this *new beginning*, the patterns of interaction between the pastor and the congregation are established, the norms of their life together are set; first impressions solidify into lasting attitudes. To some extent, these patterns and impressions grow out of the residue of the congregation's relationship with the former pastor—especially if feelings were not addressed and therefore remain unresolved. If the congregation's confidence is shaken, people may relate to their new pastor as their savior. These patterns and impressions are also shaped by the spirit with which the pastor enters the new ministry. While the congregation may have lost its former pastor months ago and be ready for a new beginning, the new pastor and family may have moved only weeks ago and may still be grieving. During this new beginning, the congregation has extra energy and people willing to support the new pastor. Ideally, the new pastor employs this energy and enthusiasm in crucial areas of the congregation's life to ensure the congregation's most viable future, rather than expending it on the pastor's favorite programs or changes that make the pastor comfortable in the new setting.

HOLY AND ACTIVE LISTENING

A departing pastor has the daunting task of appropriately listening to people's pain and grief over the loss that he or she caused. Avoiding these conversations short-circuits the congregation's grief process. Remaining totally open and receptive, however, leaves the pastor depressed and fatigued. Departing pastors therefore undertake a difficult balancing act, which is made easier when they enlist a pastoral mentor with whose help they come to terms with their feelings, a person who prevents them from falling.

The pastor in an interim period listens for the unspoken pain that underlies the obvious change; even difficult pastorates can develop loyal members. The pastor also attends to the congregation's fragility. A consultant observed, "While change is necessary, and in fact precipitates the arrival of the interim, for many folks there is a kind of catatonia that arises, as though if one more thing changes, they will shatter like glass." Knowing that pastoral transitions do not always happen under positive circumstances, interim pastors listen for boundary violations, relationship issues, and theological differences with the congregation to help the congregation respond to and address any problems.

For the new pastor, the congregation's history provides the most accurate picture of the present. Pastors begin to learn about a congregation by studying the parish profile. In conversations they pay attention to those parts of the congregation's history that people remember and pass on. They listen for stories about the congregation's beginnings; the leaders or heroes that are remembered; "days of glory;" what people recall about crisis and turmoil; people's hopes, dreams, and expectations, usually associated with church building; and key players in the congregation, some of whom are still around.[3] Pastors study how the congregation's history affects its behavior. Pastors also study their own history and the ways it influences their behavior. They are then able to compare the two to uncover any hunches they might have about the dynamics of the new relationship. Pastors keep track of things that surprise them as clues to areas where expectations are in conflict; they reflect on surprises to discover miscommunication.

New pastors ask judicatory leaders about their expectations of this congregation and their ministry there. Judicatory leaders who say they have no expectations are not in touch with their own agendas. Most important, pastors find out if any immediate conflict needs to be handled upon their arrival. To avoid being taken in by a faction, new pastors listen to make sure that changes requested by a particular group are needed, wanted, and supported before implementing them. They attend to the congregation's relationship with the former pastor by discerning the nature of that relationship and looking for the stages of grief in the congregation. Once the congregation works through its grief, members will expect to have the same kind of relationship with their new pastor. Pastors monitor shifts in power that result from their arrival. As people who more clearly reflect the new pastor's age, thinking, lifestyle, theology, and mode of operation naturally come into power, people who held positions of power during the tenure of the former pastor, whether by supporting or opposing that pastor, experience a change in their influence. These shifts occur naturally but can be handled with conscious intention.

BIBLICAL STORIES AND IMAGES

- Philippians 1:3-6: Paul tells the people, "I thank my God for you" for sharing in the gospel, and expresses confidence that God will continue to do good works through them. Congregations in every stage of a pastoral transition need to hear this praise and confidence.
- Joshua 24:1-27: In working out the covenant between God and Israel, Joshua reviews the people's history and helps the people to focus on the task at hand and the decisions they need to make.
- John 14:18-27: Jesus' promise to not leave the disciples orphaned, to come to them, and to send the Holy Spirit speaks to anxiety about being abandoned, left behind, and overwhelmed by too much change. Jesus' promise also helps the congregation get ready for something completely different and provides a way to get there from here.

PREPARING TRANSITIONAL SERMONS

During a pastoral transition, preaching the gospel shows the congregation what is primary and constant. Departing pastors may be tempted to use preaching to provide details of the pending pastoral transition. The congregation's shock and the initial phase of grief make it impossible for members to process this information, however. Departing preachers helpfully communicate their resignation and say good-bye by framing the end of their ministry in the congregation in terms of death and resurrection. They name the deaths of relationships, roles, functions, and responsibilities, and even the death of the special bond that this pastor and congregation share. Pastors then assure congregations that, in Christ, it is a life-giving experience to face our anxiety, sadness, and fear; we become more whole. The congregation needs to hear themes of continuity in the church (including the greater church), church leadership's transcending individual leaders, God's sovereign control, the faithfulness of God, and hope and vision for the future. Sermons that strongly affirm the congregation and reflect on the congregation's shared ministry are meaningful. Preachers might remind the congregation's members that they are the church and that it is important for everyone to be present and active amid the change. This kind of preaching assures the congregation that the church will continue after this pastor leaves, that God is greater than any pastor, and that pastors are all links in a chain of sharing the gospel in that place. The congregation is then able to look forward and recognize the ways God is working within the congregation, calling them to a new place in their mission as part of God's family, and in the life of the pastor, calling that pastor to a new place and a different part of God's family. Both in and out of the pulpit, preachers model this kind of closure.

The interim preacher assures the members that God loves them and, if appropriate, that the interim pastor is there to love them. During a pastoral vacancy, the congregation wants to know that whoever serves as its pastor at any given time will not abandon the members. An interim pastor described the task of preaching as "telling the congregation that you love them, demonstrating that you love them, and then preaching good theology." *Good theology* assures the congregation that, while no one can be absolutely sure what will happen with any given pastor, God will be with the congregation in everything that happens, including a pastoral change that feels sudden and unexpected. Good theology helps the individual and the community experience God's continuity and creativity in their midst. The interim preacher then helps the congregation claim its own creative continuity and envision its future life under the leadership of another pastor. The interim might ask, "Where has the congregation come from and where does it want to go?" Encouraging this vision helps the congregation imagine the kind of leader that it needs. Again, the interim pastor might ask, "What will we need from our next pastor to do the mission that God calls us to do?"

The first sermon of any new pastor attracts curious listeners. Everyone wants to know what this pastor has to say. Many people come to some firm conclusion about their new pastor on the basis of the first sermon and worship service. This is especially true of parishioners who see their pastor only occasionally or from a distance. People look for clues that the preacher genuinely cares about them. They also look for the pastor to demonstrate personal and theological authenticity. The pastor's preaching must match the way he or she lives and relates.

Preachers resist the temptation to tell the congregation everything they know. References to the former parish will be tolerated only for a short while. Clergy might take the opportunity to describe how bewildering it is to begin, how much they value the ministry, and how honored they are to be called as pastor. This kind of sermon can set the tone for at least the first year of ministry. The new pastor might preach resurrection and death. He or she first celebrates the new beginning of ministry as a resurrection, God's gift of new life. The preacher then distinguishes this new life from the old life. New life means that both pastor and congregation will experience change, unmet expectations, and opportunities to do things in new ways. New life means that, by God's grace, this pastor and congregation are creating something never done before. As it was for the first disciples, new life is both exciting and terrifying for us. Like the first disciples, the pastor and congregation will be open to God's Spirit and open with each other. In subsequent sermons, new pastors might share their "call story" and tell how they understand the core doctrines or basic beliefs of the faith. People pay particular attention to the words the preacher chooses. New pastors gain confidence as leaders in the new congregation, and the congregation gets to know the new pastor in a "safe" way.

ANCHORED IN GOD

Departing, interim, and arriving pastors all need to understand clearly their theology of call and their own grief. Pastors convinced that they are responding to a divine call report relying on God to walk with them and trusting God to take care of them and their families, the church they are leaving, and whatever lies ahead. Some pastors, particularly those in a call system rather than an appointive system, end up confusing their grief over their former parish with making a wrong decision to accept a call elsewhere. Reflecting on how one handled past transitions, whether with congregations or other people, reveals both how a person grieves and the way one wants to be regarded and remembered. Whether coming or going, pastors experience sadness over separating from people and a congregation that have been significant; they also experience a mixture of anticipation and fear related to the new congregation. Pastors may have real concerns for their immediate families and how they will make the transition to a new place.

Departing pastors need to be open and candid with people about what they experience emotionally and spiritually, while remaining open and receptive to where the people are emotionally. Avoiding these feelings does not work because after leaving a congregation a pastor continues to deal with unexpressed grief, which may emerge in unexpected ways. Failure to address these feelings causes the pastor to function as a victim, rendering a healthy ministry with new people virtually impossible. At some level, pastors desire to control what happens in the congregation after their departure. They must let go of this influence if they are to "leave well." Specifically, clergy must let go of pastoral roles; hanging on to a previous pastoral role is a bid at immortality and an attempt to be indispensable to people so that we live forever in their hearts. The celebration of the pastor's ministry helps the pastor and congregation to let go of the ministry they have shared and to begin a new relationship, though for the pastor it often feels like a funeral with the deceased present to hear the eulogies.

Arriving pastors will continue to experience grief over their former parishes. They may feel abandoned by church judicatories, which often consider their work complete. The pastor's confidence may be shaken, either by the circumstances of their departure or by the challenges of the new parish. Pastors will certainly feel incompetent because they do not know people, relationships, where things are, and how things are done in this congregation. They will also feel overwhelmed as they receive great quantities of information very quickly. Arriving pastors remember that this congregation had a significant ministry before their arrival. As new pastors consider making changes, they distinguish between preferences, changes in program or worship that represent a model or ideal, and changes in norms and practices that are essential for the congregation's continued health and life. They enlist others to address practices that drag the parish down. Pastors also relieve stress by cultivating the ability to listen to stories about the former pastor and to feel neither threatened by the former pastor's gifts nor judgmental of the former pastor's shortcomings and mistakes.

A BOOK TO READ

Roy M. Oswald, James M. Heath, and Ann W. Heath, *Beginning Ministry Together: The Alban Handbook for Clergy Transitions* (Bethesda, Md.: Alban Institute, 2003).

CHAPTER 7

A NEW VISION FOR MISSION

A *vision for mission* is "a clear mental image of a preferable future imparted by God to [God's] chosen servants and is based on an accurate understanding of God, self, and circumstances."[1] Practically, a vision for mission helps a congregation to direct, align, and inspire actions on the part of large numbers of people. Without a vision, efforts at transformation can easily dissolve into confusing, incompatible, and time-consuming projects that lack direction.[2] One paragraph is long enough to state a congregation's vision. The vision statement avoids both theological language and triviality. It uses an image to convey its message; it is simple enough to be remembered; and it is specific enough to give direction. The best way to find examples of current vision statements is to look online for congregational home pages; those searching might begin with congregations of their own faith tradition or from their local community.

A vision for mission is bigger than a program or a plan. Programs and plans are tools that a congregation uses to fulfill or, better, to live into its vision. A vision is a clear mental image that encapsulates a forward-looking change. The congregation understands its vision to be a call from God to this particular gathering of God's people. While all things are possible for God, the vision is realistic because it is based on an accurate understanding of God, the congregation, and the circumstances that the congregation seeks to address. In this way, the vision makes sense to the congregation. Though well-defined, a congregation's vision remains flexible enough to respond to both factors beyond the congregation's control and God's Spirit at work among the people.

Vision is not created in a vacuum but is shaped by many factors. For example, the congregation's denomination or faith tradition has an essential voice. The faith tradition provides the congregation's mission. The congregation's *mission statement* articulates the theological underpinnings of its life.[3] The mission statement defines the key ministry objectives of the congregation or faith community. Many Christian congregations find their mission in the Great Commission (Matt. 28:19-20) or the sermon Jesus preached in the synagogue at Nazareth (Luke 4:18-19). A mission statement describes the congregation's "being." A vision statement describes the congregation's "doing." The vision clarifies the specific direction and activities that the congregation will pursue to carry out its mission. It brings the congregation's mission to bear on the contextual realities the congregation is called to address, and on the neighborhood or region in this specific time. The vision is not the only way the congregation might carry out its mission; the vision is the way the congregation discerns and decides to carry out its mission. Although the congregation's vision changes with time and circumstance, its mission remains constant.

THE NATURE OF THE TRANSITION

Claiming a new vision for mission is one way a congregation chooses to respond to a change and transition. When the congregation's life progresses as expected, the members often feel that they are fulfilling the congregation's vision for mission. When a change occurs, particularly in its environment, a congregation may conclude that it needs a new vision to respond to the change. One pastor described the claiming of a new vision for mission as "chasing a hurricane" because the congregation runs toward the change to understand it, rather than waiting for the change to strike and reacting to it.

The change that creates the need for a new vision can be sudden and unexpected. A congregation that receives a bequest of $2 million or loses its building to fire experiences a sudden change that requires a new vision. A congregation in a changing neighborhood, where the majority of potential new members prefer a type of church different from the churches already there, is frequently confronted by an unexpected change that calls for new vision. Alternatively, the need for a new vision is a normal part of the congregation's life cycle, either as the congregation moves to the next stage in its organizational life cycle or chooses between renewal and death.[4]

At its best, claiming a new vision revitalizes the congregation and every area of its life. At the same time, a new vision brings pain and loss as the congregation releases its old vision and the life that flowed from it. Embracing a new vision is frequently a slower and longer process than pastors expect and desire; clergy must remain patient as they wait for the vision to take shape and become established. Patience should not be confused with passivity. Some congregations perpetually engage in visioning as a means of maintaining the status quo and postponing the hard work of ministry. Other congregations create vision statements and quickly deposit them in a file cabinet or on a shelf, never to be seen again.

HOLY AND ACTIVE LISTENING

Holy and active listening is especially important during the liminal strand of this transition, when the congregation first creates and then tests its new vision for mission. During the formation of the vision statement, members of the congregation might be asked, "Where do you see our congregation in 10 years?" The pastor and other leaders could interview the congregation's neighbors and community leaders to learn how the congregation might best serve its context. As it gathers this information, the congregation will ask, "What does the Bible say our congregational life should be about?" Exploring this question could be the focus of both preaching and Bible study. Listening to form a vision for mission can take a year. People need to be given time and freedom to be creative. In the end, the congregation's vision arises as God speaks through a synthesis and not a single voice.

Thomas Troeger contends that visionary preachers know that they can be wrong in understanding how Christ's mission in the world is changing, so they test their visions with the church that gathers. Troeger reminds us that, since God alone is holy and because Christ not only moves in the individual heart but also among the community of faith, preachers have the grace to apply "the hermeneutic of suspicion" to their own utterances in the name of God.[5] Before a preacher proclaims God's vision for the congregation, he or she tests that vision with the congregation. George Barna, author of *The Power of Vision: How You Can Capture and Apply God's Vision for Your Ministry*,[6] suggests several questions that congregations might use to test their visions. I summarize them here:

- If the congregation is invited to participate in a reasonable ministry opportunity, is the vision statement specific enough to justify declining the invitation for reasons relevant to the congregation's ministry?
- Does the vision statement highlight the congregation's uniqueness by differentiating it from neighboring churches?
- Does the vision statement identify the target audience to which the congregation hopes to minister? Does it provide parameters that prevent the congregation from trying to be everything to everyone?
- Does the vision statement provide a clear direction for the future?
- Are members—active or inactive—excited about the vision?

In *Moving Beyond Church Growth*, Mark Olson provides questions that lift up a different perspective on ministry.[7]

- What does the vision statement say about the frequency and character of the congregation's gathering? How central are story and table to the vision? What stories are told as the people gather around the table?
- According to the vision statement, how is the congregation rooted in the Bible? How does the congregation understand the nature and place of Scripture in its life?
- How essential is visitation to the vision statement?
- According to the vision statement, what is the nature of congregational and individual prayer life? Who does the congregation invite into community through its prayers?
- According to the vision statement, what is the congregation offering widows, orphans, strangers, and all who are in need?

Perhaps the best way the preacher can listen to the congregation is to state the vision in five minutes or less and listen for people's reaction, understanding, and level of interest.[8] Congregational leaders will also want to be attentive to the ways children respond to what is happening in church. Do high-school youth come to church? Do young adults come to church when they are home from college? Most important, parishioners must accept and claim the vision as their own creation and not something imposed.

BIBLICAL STORIES AND IMAGES

- Exodus 3 and 4: Both the call of Moses and Moses' need for Aaron illustrate that God uses the ordinary to create the extraordinary. God's vision becomes real through limited human beings. This story also shows that leading people into God's vision is a shared endeavor.
- Acts 1: Jesus' ascension and promise that the disciples will bear witness to him encourages healthy risk. Where does God ask us to go? What does God give us to get there?
- Isaiah 56:7: "My house shall be called a house of prayer for all peoples." What would it mean for this congregation to be a place where God brings all people, makes them joyful, and accepts their offerings?

PREPARING TRANSITIONAL SERMONS

The preacher serves as the communal voice of the people of God by leading the process and naming what emerges as the community of faith discerns, articulates, and enacts its vision for mission. The preacher does not surprise the congregation with the vision he or she arrived at. Rather, preaching invites and involves the congregation in the process. Preachers help the congregation embrace both the vision and the process as long-term. A consultant observed, "If you don't acknowledge that visioning is a long journey, you will leave people tarrying in the end zone while you preach from the launch site." The mixed metaphor reveals a deeper truth; more than being in different places, the pastor and congregation will be pursuing different purposes. The content of the sermon reflects the substance of the visioning process and, ultimately, the vision. The questions asked in the process and the emerging vision statement might serve as a lens through which the preacher views the biblical text.

Creating an image is more effective than either discussing a concept or proclaiming a slogan. The image reflects both the things that hold the congregation fast to God's grace and the things that move and shape the congregation to create a picture of God's action in our lives. The image helps people reorganize their perceptions, experience, and faith in a new or alternative way. Preachers use vivid language to draw the image in people's minds to expand and enlighten their world of meaning.

More than anything else, preaching a vision for mission inspires the congregation to see God's future for the congregation. Thomas Troeger contends that the task of visionary preachers is to enlighten and expand the landscape of the heart, to broaden the capacity of human beings to extend the grace and compassion of God to others.[9] To broaden their capacity to extend God's grace and compassion, people must experience God's grace and compassion themselves. The vision is therefore always understood as "good news" that flows from the gospel. Preachers make a bold, clear, and unambiguous proclamation that is meaningful to these hearers on this occasion. Rather than diluting and even denying the Christian claim, preachers consider how it opens us up to the pluralistic worlds of others. They reframe faith so that it addresses the current reality. Rather than abandoning tradition, preachers modify it to meet the current reality by claiming people's cherished and sacred stories, memories, customs, and symbols and by drawing upon those portions of Christian practice that make sense of our experience.

Preaching a vision for mission is obviously change oriented. The preacher seeks to reveal God's promised future; the preacher proclaims resurrection as "something greater than returning to the life that once was."[10] At the same time, the challenge must be realistic both about what God is calling the congregation to do and what the congregation can accomplish. Inasmuch as the congregation's self-realization is essential for the vision to materialize, preachers challenge people without chastising. A consultant observed, "We may need to hit hard but not hard enough to break." The emphasis, then, is on empowering the congregation to name, claim, and live into its vision. Congregations are motivated by God's word and not the preacher's. Preachers therefore show how the vision is modeled on the lives of biblical characters. They also use Scripture to give courage, resolve, and energy. They relate the vision to the hearers' everyday thoughts, questions, and activities; they use their personal experience as inspiration but not content.

After the congregation creates, tests, and adopts its vision statement, preachers regularly incorporate the vision statement into the sermon. Short phrases and repetition work better than reading the statement in its entirety. This is uttering "blended speech" and not quoting a document. The preacher might occasionally tell the story of the congregation's vision and then invite the congregation to live the story. Most important, the preacher repeats, reminds, and reinforces. A single sermon will not suffice. As an integral part of the congregation's life, the vision is an integral and ongoing part of preaching and part of a larger ministry of implementation.

ANCHORED IN GOD

Consultants suggest three ways a preacher remains anchored in God during a visioning process. First, the preacher respects the congregation. Thomas Troeger invites visionary preachers to treat the congregation and its customs with the respect they would show upon entering someone's house for a meal. Troeger observes that preachers are guests in a household of faith that has seen preachers come and go; preachers need to honor the ways of that household before they attempt any change.[11]

Second, preachers separate their ego from the congregation's vision. They resist the temptation to equate the congregation's vision with their own vision for ministry. Preachers avoid fear and anxiety about achieving the goal or change. The preacher's task is to help the congregation take its next step toward entering more fully into God's reign. The pressure to succeed, which comes from the preacher, the congregation, and the greater church, makes this perspective very difficult to maintain.

Third, preachers cannot vision by themselves. Since the vision comes from God, the preacher is in regular conversation with God. Since the vision is for the congregation, he or she brings the congregation's key players on board. Rather than seeing them as an additional burden, the preacher embraces collaboration and partnership as gifts from God and the means through which God speaks.

A BOOK TO READ

George Barna, *The Power of Vision: How You Can Capture and Apply God's Vision for Your Ministry* (Ventura, Calif.: Gospel Light, 1992).

CHAPTER 8

SIGNIFICANT CHANGE IN MEMBERSHIP OR FINANCIAL GIVING

"When it comes to congregations, size is never simply about size," quipped a pastor familiar with the ups and the downs of fluctuating worship attendance. A congregation's size influences, in predictable ways, its financial giving, its organization, and its ways of operating. In fact, congregations of a similar size ought to share a common leadership structure and relationship style. A *leadership structure* is the way a congregation *governs* its life; a *relationship style* is the way members relate to each other. The literature in congregational studies describes four types of congregations, identified by their average worship attendance. Those with similar attendance figures share similarities in their leadership structure and membership style.[1]

A *family church* has an average worship attendance of one to 50 people; it incorporates new members the way a family does, through birth, marriage, and adoption. The pastor functions as the family chaplain—preaching, leading worship, caring for the sick, opening meetings with prayer, and staying out of the way of the patriarchs and matriarchs, those "moms" and "dads" who run the congregation. Clergy are not the chief executives and resident religious authorities in family churches. Pastors exercise leadership as consultants to the patriarchs and matriarchs, recognizing that when those parental figures decide against an idea, it is finished.

The average worship attendance of a *pastoral church* is 51 to 150. Members join pastoral churches based on the relationship they develop with the pastor. People expect to have their spiritual needs met through a personal relationship with the pastor. Growth depends on the popularity and effectiveness of the pastor. The pastor is the hub of the congregational wheel. The congregation's leadership circle consists of the pastor and a small cadre of key lay leaders. Its power and effectiveness depend on good communication with the pastor and the pastor's ability to delegate authority, assign responsibility, and recognize the accomplishments of others. When the pastor does not possess these skills, this central figure can weaken the entire structure. Pastors in this situation find themselves overworked, isolated, exhausted, and attacked by other leaders as the harmony of the leadership circle degenerates. Pastoral congregations value the sense of family in which everyone knows everyone else. When their average worship attendance rises beyond about 130 or 150, these congregations begin to get nervous because people do not know everyone.[2] Clergy also feel stressed because it is impossible to know more than 150 people in depth.

While some authors place the range of attendance for the *program church* at 151 to 350, others push the upper number as high as 1,000. As the name suggests, people are primarily attracted by the congregation's programs, including activities for children and adults, study, music, education, fellowship, and support. Pastors of program churches spend time and attention planning with lay leaders to ensure the highest quality of programming possible. The pastor works with these leaders to recruit people to head smaller ministries; to train, supervise and evaluate them; and to keep their morale high. The pastor steps back from direct ministry to coordinate and support the volunteers who offer the ministry. Pastors give high priority to the pastoral and spiritual needs of lay leaders so that programs do not suffer.

Depending on which authors you read, the *corporate church* has an average worship attendance of 351 (or 1,001) and higher. Corporate churches possess the human, financial, and physical resources for high-quality ministries that rival major secular corporations; and they operate in a similar manner. To ensure the quality of Sunday morning worship, the head of staff spends more time than other clergy preparing to preach and lead worship. Few parishioners know this pastor well, but the role does not require it. The senior pastor functions as a symbol of unity and stability in a complicated congregational life. This pastor's personal ministry is devoted to promoting staff harmony.

While a congregation's size is numerically measured by its average worship attendance, this number is only part of the equation. Rather than the numbers, the way a congregation governs its life and the ways its members relate to each other determine the congregation's actual type. Thus, a congregation's attitude about its sense of community and the organization of its common life matters as much as its numbers.

THE NATURE OF THE TRANSITION

Congregations grow emotionally and organizationally, as well as numerically and physically, to welcome and make a place for new members. If congregations do not grow, they will not have the physical, emotional, and numerical room for more people. Either an increase or a decrease in size necessitates a congregational transition from one congregational type to another. Whether the congregation needs to increase its size to provide emotional and numerical room for new members or to adapt to a sharp decrease in the number of members, the congregation's main task is to change its leadership structure and relationship style to those appropriate to the type of congregation that will emerge from the transition.

These transitions have been called redefinition, redevelopment, and rebirth.[3] A transition in size is actually a matter of changing the culture of the congregation. At least to a degree, the congregation must give up its old identity, leadership structure, and relationship style and claim new ones. Thus, the goal of the transition is to make sure that the congregation's size, leadership structure, and relationship style are congruent. This transition is different from and precedes efforts toward numerical growth. That is, the congregation must begin to adapt the organization structure and relational style of the congregation it is becoming even before its worship attendance changes.

A congregation might experience six transitions related to size as it moves from one type of congregation to another.[4] As a congregation moves from *family* to *pastoral* size, the patriarchs and matriarchs lose self-esteem and power. Often, the congregation's reluctance to break up and expand the family comes into conflict with financial realism about its need to grow. Unseasoned preachers frequently take the congregation's resistance to change personally.

Conversely, when a congregation moves from *pastoral* to *family* size, it experiences a real loss of self-esteem because the congregation feels it no longer operates like a real church. The congregation wonders and worries over whether the change will bring slow death or something new and alive. The congregation must find ways of forming partnerships to do things it can no longer do on its own, such as youth ministry. The congregation must also decide how to care for a beloved building and determine what facilities it really needs.

When congregations move from *pastoral* size to *program* size, their members experience two significant losses. First, people lose ready access to their pastor, who has less time to spend with individuals and must adopt a less spontaneous schedule. The congregation also loses that family feeling—everyone knowing everyone else and the church functioning as a single community. As people no longer know everyone else personally, they become concerned with the process by which volunteers are selected, equipped, and authorized to lead programs. Coordinating a variety of ministries and communicating among them becomes more important. Finally, congregations must establish ways of ensuring democratic decision making and an appropriate sense of unity.

Flipping the coin, when a congregation moves from *program* size to *pastoral* size, the transition is still concerned with reshaping expectations. As the congregation focuses on a few central strengths, it remains attentive to feelings of loss and grief for everything it gives up. The pastor may experience loss of both status and satisfaction as a simpler form of ministry becomes necessary. Simplifying the worship and education schedule without initiating a cycle of decline, streamlining the volunteer structure, and embracing a modest congregational lifestyle are the difficult issues faced by congregations making this transition.

As a congregation moves from *program* size to *corporate* size, it steps up to a higher level of expectations. The pastor must embrace a more symbolic role, which can be lonelier and spiritually more hazardous for both the shepherd and the flock. People's primary connection to the church becomes the small groups they belong to. As the "big picture" becomes more important, making changes becomes akin to making a sharp turn with an ocean liner.

As a congregation moves from *corporate* size to *program* size, it must come to terms with its need to relinquish status and reject the temptation to keep up appearances. In other words, the congregation must honestly face decline. The way a congregation uses endowment funds provides an important indication of how that congregation is dealing with its decline. Does the congregation spend the gifts of the past or consolidate programs and undertake a new approach to evangelism? As a congregation moves from corporate size to program size, the pastor needs to develop a more collegial style of ministry.

HOLY AND ACTIVE LISTENING

The first thing preachers ought to listen for is the type of congregation they serve. They should determine whether it is a family, pastoral, program, or corporate congregation. Obviously, the pastor examines records of the congregation's average worship attendance and financial giving, readily available in annual reports. With these statistics in mind, the preacher attends to three other factors—the congregation's leadership structure, its relationship style, and its expectations of the pastor—to determine whether the congregation's culture is congruent with its size type.

Second, preachers consider the reasons attendance or giving is changing, or why these need to change. Is the change the planned-for and desired result of efforts at evangelism or a stewardship campaign? Is the change the unanticipated result of variables beyond the congregation's control, such as company layoffs moving people away or the construction of new housing near the church bringing people in? Preachers observe the change to determine who is coming and going and why.

Third, the pastor inventories the congregation's beliefs and feelings about its present identity, the change that is occurring or will occur, and the new identity that will result. Whether they are growing or downsizing, congregations hold to deeply ingrained assumptions about what constitutes a dynamic church and what effective pastors do. The inflexibility of these expectations is a primary cause of the lack of congruence between a congregation's size and type and, more important, the congregation's malfunctioning. Preachers therefore listen for their congregants' convictions about how a church should function and feel, as well as what "good pastors" do. In the course of the transition, leaders monitor whether the congregation's attitudes, expectations, leadership structure, and relational style are appropriately shifting with changes in the congregation's size. Otherwise, a transition in size may lead to a crisis of identity as the congregation recognizes that it is no longer what it wants to be or feels it should be. The congregation might be asked, "Who are we as God's people, individually and as a congregation? Do you consider the change in size that is occurring in our congregation a blessing or a problem? Why?"

Most important perhaps, the preacher listens for the reasons the congregation wants to grow. While a congregation may express a sincere desire to share the gospel, its desire to grow may result from other considerations. Heightened expectations for high-quality facilities, staff, and ministries lead many congregations to want to grow to increase their operating budgets. The increasing cost of clergy compensation and a worsening shortage of pastors, particularly clergy who feel called to serve smaller congregations, leads many congregations to conclude that they have no choice but to grow in order to survive. Unfortunately, these motives are insufficient to guarantee that congregations will successfully make the transition from one size type to another. In fact, attempts at transitions in congregational size fail more often than they succeed.

For example, the transition to a program-size church, the most appropriate response to pressures on pastoral-size congregations, may be resisted by clergy, leaders, and members alike because they all prefer simplicity to complexity. These transitions are often marked by pain, resistance, sabotage, and inevitable membership disruption.[5] In these situations, preachers listen for anything the congregation considers "nonnegotiable"—those people, practices, and possessions the congregation cannot or will not give up or change. The congregation's "nonnegotiables" may include staff people, worship or fellowship practices, and even the building. Refusing to give them up may escalate a sense of decline and undermine the vitality that could be developed.

BIBLICAL STORIES AND IMAGES

- Exodus 16:3: The entire congregation of Israel complains against Moses and Aaron and longs for Egypt; the people express their fear that they will die in the wilderness. This classic text for the liminal strand of transition provides a powerful way of giving voice to what the congregation experiences as it moves from one size type to another.

- Numbers 10:33-11:9: God hears and responds to Israel's complaints by providing manna, quail, God's spirit on 70 elders, and support for Israel's leader.
- 1 Corinthians 12:27-31: Paul compares the church to the body of Christ. Just as the human body grows and changes, so does the church.
- Acts: Examples of different size types in the New Testament church include the family church "gathered together in one place" (2:1), congregations forming by their relationship with Paul and Barnabas (13:43-52), and the pastoral church becoming a program church (6:1-7). These images could be used separately or together.

PREPARING TRANSITIONAL SERMONS

Even though Christ's church changes, Jesus Christ does not. Preachers herald the good news of God's unchanging love as the foundation that frees the congregation to consider changing its personality and culture. Preachers help their congregations understand that, as living organisms, congregations change. Preachers also help their congregations recognize that, every time there is a considerable shift in size and giving, congregations must change their behavior and expectations.

Preachers help the congregation identify and name the reasons for growth and change so that the congregation comes to regard these reasons as a faithful response to the gospel. As part of this proclamation, the preacher disabuses the congregation of any inappropriate reasons for change. For example, many congregations want more members so that more people are on board to do the work. In reality, the proportion of worship-only members grows as the numerical size of the congregation increases. Greater complexity allows for greater anonymity. As a result, larger congregations may have more members without a corresponding level of active participation.[6] Similarly, while Sunday morning may be enough to attract new people, it is not enough to keep them. Assimilating new members requires that people become involved in worship and two other activities.

Finally, the preacher honestly names the costs of change in ways that free and empower the congregation to choose its future. Unless the pastor, congregational leaders, and the people are willing to make the sometimes

painful changes needed, the congregation will not change its identity, expectations, leadership structure, and relational style. More important, the
congregation will minister less effectively. The preacher might ask, "Do we
want growth knowing that growth will mean change?"

ANCHORED IN GOD

First, pastors in growing and declining congregations must examine their
own convictions about what faithful and effective pastors do, and how these
strong beliefs may affect the congregation. For example, pastors may keep
pastoral-size churches from growing to program size because they firmly
believe that pastors are ineffective unless they relate in profound and personal ways to every member of the congregation. Realistically, 150 people
are all the church members that one person can handle. On the other hand,
preachers may thwart change by implementing ideas, ministries, policies
and strategies that worked well in a congregation of one size but fail in one
of a smaller or larger size. Second, pastors cultivate self-differentiation and
guard against inappropriately internalizing either credit for the
congregation's growth or blame for its decline. If the pastor commits either
of these errors, he or she will eventually experience failure, rejection, disil-
lusionment, and frustration. Finally, pastors may find themselves in a lose-
lose situation when they fail to meet the competing expectations laid upon
them by the congregation, which wants growth without change. Pastors
therefore constantly seek God's will for the congregation, leading the members to do the same as they sort through competing expectations.

A BOOK TO READ

Beth Ann Gaede, ed., *Size Transitions in Congregations* (Bethesda, Md.: Alban
Institute, 2001).

CHAPTER 9

COMPLETION OF THE CONGREGATION'S MINISTRY

Closing a congregation can be a faithful response to the gospel, a courageous witness to the resurrection, and an opportunity to release resources for new ministry. All living things, including congregations, have a life span and will eventually die. Faithful congregations do not survive; they fulfill the mission God gives them. When a congregation has completed its mission, it either claims a new mission or moves toward ending its life. Claiming a new mission and revitalizing an existing congregation is a long, hard process. Before entering into this difficult and often painful work, congregations should seriously consider the possibility of closing, of completing their ministry, as well as every other option that the congregation may initially dismiss as out of bounds. "Eventually, as various scenarios are explored, the congregation will ask, 'To what ministry is God calling us?' Specifically asking, 'Why not close?' raises the possibility that God calls some churches to close."[1]

Ellen Morseth—a staff-mentor at Worshipful-Work: Center for Transforming Religious Leadership, an ecumenical ministry that integrates spirituality and administration in church governance—suggests that rather than deciding a congregation's future on the basis of financial considerations, dwindling worship attendance, or a shortage of pastors, we might invite the congregation to approach decision making as spiritual discernment. Morseth encourages congregations to ask, "What might God want for this particular congregation with its unique history and identity?"[2] By prayerfully seeking God's yearning for the congregation, people will be freed to look beyond institutional survival, to seek God's larger vision, and to pray for God's guidance to move the church forward, by whatever means

God chooses. Instead of making a quick, practical, or sentimental decision, congregations can approach the possibility of completing a congregation's ministry using study, prayer, and spiritual discernment to provide significant time to ponder God's intentions.

THE NATURE OF THE TRANSITION

Often, the change that causes a congregation to understand its ministry as completed is the congregation's recognition that it cannot continue to function. Even after simplifying its structure, cutting expenses, and curtailing activities, the congregation possesses insufficient resources, interest, and activity to maintain ministry, let alone attract new members. This awareness comes slowly and is armored in strong denial. People counter facts with professions of faith that God will do something miraculous. While the leadership is demoralized, stressed, and exhausted, members who come only to worship services believe that everything is fine. The *ending* the congregation needs to make is recognizing and accepting that the congregation can no longer function.

The *liminal strand* is the process of deciding the congregation's future. Ellen Morseth describes this decision making as a process of spiritual discernment that consists of nine steps.[3] First, the congregation *frames* the issue by formulating a question addressed to God. A group such as the congregational council works to articulate the question before it is presented to the congregation, where it is refined. The question must be succinct and clear so that everyone understands it. If the question is not addressed to God, people will talk about and answer it in terms of their own desires, despite their good intentions. Returning again and again to "the God question" keeps the congregation centered on God's will and desire.

Second, the congregation seeks to *ground the question* by creating a guiding principle that is so important to the life of the congregation that it is nonnegotiable. The guiding principle is informed by the congregation's values and may be part of its vision statement. One congregation unanimously agreed that whatever it decided must be a faithful witness to the gospel. Grounding the question sets boundaries. Eventually, all options that surface during discernment will be judged via the guiding principle.

In the third step of the process, *rooting and shedding*, the congregation works to root the question in faith and shed its own desires. Rooting involves telling stories from Scripture and the denomination's tradition, as well as stories about this congregation, that inform the question being asked of God. Getting rooted in tradition helps the congregation form a corporate memory. Once everyone knows the story in all its depth, then biblical and theological reflection on that story helps the congregation understand itself, its priorities, and its values. Shedding is the continuous effort to be liberated from our own desires. "Shedding is a time of coming to holy indifference about anything other than God's yearning."[4]

Step four, *listening*, does not happen just once but is threaded throughout the discernment process. This step is covered in more detail below.

In step five, *exploring*, the congregation looks at every possibility through the lens of its guiding principle to see God's preferred future. Exploring is the congregation's process of seeing dreams and visions beyond practical solutions. Once options emerge, the congregation seeks to *improve* them, the sixth step. The congregation works with each option until it is constructed and articulated as well as it can be. The congregation's story and guiding principle help the congregation improve its options.

Next, the congregation carefully and prayerfully *weighs* each option to determine its driving force. Is God the driving force, or is the congregation preferring what is easiest, least painful, or least costly? Once it has weighed its options, the congregation is ready to *close* its time of discernment by deciding which option seems to be that for which God most yearns. The congregation must decide how this decision will be made. Although a congregational vote may be constitutionally required, that is not always the best way to proceed. The decision may be welcomed or resisted by the congregation, which will *rest* with the decision before it becomes official. During this rest, members attend to how the decision is setting with them.

HOLY AND ACTIVE LISTENING

Leaders listen so they can give considered attention to every voice that needs to be heard and that will be affected by whatever the congregation decides. These voices include people within and outside the congregation, voices the congregation does not want to hear (such as church judicatories), Scripture, the Holy Spirit, feelings as well as facts, unspoken voices (such as the voices of the faithful departed), and the voice of resistance.

Leaders listen to distinguish whether the congregation wants to grow and change or feels it *should* or *must* grow and change to survive. As in all size transitions, many congregations want growth without change. They desire to attract more people to pay the bills and share the work, but they do not want their congregation's culture to change.[5]

Leaders attend to people's feelings of loss. Four types of loss commonly occur. First, some people are so attached, even enslaved, to the church building and the memories, history, identity, and furnishings associated with that building that contemplating the congregation's end is impossible for them. Second, a congregation completing its ministry causes longtime, faithful members to confront their own mortality. For these members, the death of the church in which they have invested their lives becomes the first step in their own deaths. They are understandably concerned with how the church will minister to them at their time of death, since the congregation where they are known will no longer exist. Third, members experience the loss of their church family and weekly routine. Fourth, people lose their connection to their history and to deceased loved ones who were once church members.

Feelings of loss are accompanied by feelings of failure and unfaithfulness. Congregations that close, as well as the leaders and pastors who lead their closure, are often stigmatized. American culture associates wealth, size, influence, and longevity with success. Churches that are numerically growing and that boast large budgets are considered faithful because of their "success." Even the wider church often regards congregations that do not grow as unfaithful. This pervasive attitude inhibits congregations from seeing how God is working in their lives and leads them to feel that they are somehow unfaithful and have failed God. Given permission, people will ask, "Where is God in all this? Have we failed God? Has God failed us? Does God prefer the successful churches?"

Leaders are alert to the stages of grief in the congregation, recognizing that various members of the congregation are at different stages in their grief. Denial is strong; it leads the congregation to rewrite history to lessen its own responsibility. The congregation feels and expresses anger toward many entities, including uncontrollable circumstances and events, pastors and church judicatories, former leaders of the congregation, and God. People need permission and safe space to feel and express their anger. Desperate members bargain for more time, another chance, and greater church intervention. Some members become so depressed that they withdraw and leave; they should be given permission to do so. Acceptance comes slowly and tentatively; some people do not accept the church's closing until years after the congregation completes its ministry.

BIBLICAL IMAGES AND STORIES

- Matthew 16:24-28: Jesus' call to deny ourselves, take up our cross, and lose our life can help congregations embrace completing their ministry and sacrificing their desires for the sake of the gospel as a faithful response to the Christ.
- Matthew 18:20: Help congregations understand that, when Jesus speaks of being present where two or three gather in his name, he is giving assurance, not providing a model for congregational life.
- John 14:16: This passage, often used to proclaim the gospel to individuals and families, is equally appropriate and powerful when applied to a congregation.
- Romans 8:31-39: The assurance that nothing can separate us from the love of Christ is powerful good news to people who feel that they have been unfaithful and have failed God.
- For more suggestions, see Gaede, ed., *Ending with Hope*, 139-140.

PREPARING TRANSITIONAL SERMONS

The preacher can express the congregation's feelings and shape its consciousness so that people see the closing of their church not as a failure of mission but as a mission accomplished. Through preaching, the pastor can enable the congregation to envision the end of its life together through lenses of hope rather than despair, faithfulness rather than failure, and grace rather than condemnation.

The preacher engages the congregation in the story and history of the church in sermons and prayers. The preacher names the congregation's dilemmas, weaknesses, and limitations, and asks God's continued guidance. He or she also lifts up the congregation's strengths and opportunities. Rather than offering answers and solutions, the preacher helps the congregation to wrestle with questions of God's will and whether the congregation has the will and desire to respond.

Preachers remind the congregation that, whatever it decides, the congregation and its ministry will change. Like all living things, congregations grow, change, and eventually die. While the church of Jesus Christ is eternal, a congregations is not. Like all living things, congregations are not static. The congregation will not remain as it is indefinitely; as it changed in response to decline, so it must change if it is to grow. Regardless of what the congregation decides, the congregation as it is today will no longer exist. This change is not the result of failure but a natural part of the congregation's life and an indication that the congregation has completed its mission. Members who understand that congregations have life cycles are more likely to consider closure.

The preacher connects the congregation to the greater church and to God's ongoing mission by declaring that, when God's mission is complete in one place, the church moves to new places. He or she celebrates the times when this congregation contributed to God's mission in the world. If a church baptized and taught the faith, it participated in God's mission. The preacher then offers a vision for the congregation's future. For example, a congregation that decides to close and sell the church building might use the proceeds of the sale to help fund mission congregations elsewhere. Through this congregation's courage, faith, and sacrifice, God provides a new way for the community to contribute to God's mission. Like Jesus, a faithful community follows where God calls, even to death, to participate in God's mission.

As the congregation acknowledges that its common life is ending, the sermon reflects people's emotion and loss. The preacher spends a great deal of time talking with members about the closing and taking the pulse of the people. This is not the time for the preacher to share a vision for the future, but to listen and reflect theologically on what the people say.

When the congregation decides to complete its ministry, the preacher honestly names people's feelings of anxiety, anger, frustration, pain, relief, joy, and fear. Naming people's emotions allows those who voiced their feelings to feel heard; those who did not will be given "permission" to feel loss without shame or embarrassment. This is the time for the preacher to stand with the congregation, to let the members know that their pastor is affected as well by sharing his or her feelings. The preacher moves the congregation from legitimizing thoughts and feelings to framing these thoughts and feelings with the promise of the gospel. The key theological point is that, even when we feel most abandoned, God is present. God meets us at our darkest moment of despair. Just as God was with the congregation during times of prosperity, God is present and faithful in the time of closing. Once the preacher shows that he or she understands the congregation, it is appropriate to begin to cast a vision for the transition. While the congregation's mission of many years is complete, God gives the congregation a new mission. God calls the members to celebrate and recognize the end of the old mission and the beginning of something new.

During the time between the decision to close and the day of closing, the sermon shapes and maintains a feeling of working toward God's new mission for the congregation. This interval is also a good time to publicly address people's pastoral concerns and to assure them that they will not be forgotten by God or the church. The sermon affirms and demonstrates to the people how much they are loved, that their ministry is valued, and that God has not abandoned them. They have not failed God, and God has not left them. Even though the congregation is closing, it is a witness to the ongoing grace and mercy of God, who does not abandon God's people but brings life out of death.

As the congregation ends its ministry, the preacher helps the faithful say good-bye to everything and everyone. This is an opportunity for celebration and joy as the preacher publicly remembers the congregation's faithful ministry. This occasion is the time to recall the ways the church has carried out the mission of Jesus Christ and has been a positive force in the world. By recounting honestly rather than glossing over the past, the preacher gives people a sense of accomplishment and closure. She or he then reminds the hearers that the congregation lives on in them because the church is the people and not the building. The unique experiences and ministry of a faith community do not dissolve but remain as faithful witness to the transforming power of God in a particular place and time. The preacher also assures the congregation that, though the faith communities they may join have different histories, people, and futures, they possess the same spirit and gospel that this congregation knows and loves. By inviting the congregation to be open to the transforming power of God in those new communities, the preacher proclaims God's new beginning as the opportunity to participate in new missions of God.

ANCHORED IN GOD

The challenge to preachers is to be present to anxiety and grief, the congregation's and their own, without being overcome by them. To maintain this balance, preachers recognize the grief within and around them and get the help that is needed. Preachers combat the isolation that results from being shunned by people and other churches that do not want to be reminded of death. This kind of isolation can follow pastors throughout their careers. On the other hand, preachers might suppress their anger, become depressed, and cut themselves off from everyone else. Preachers might experience their careers as threatened because many in the church consider closing a congregation a "failure," regardless of the pastor's past accomplishments or longevity of service. Ultimately, the pastor may feel like a failure and become angry with and feel abandoned by God. In these moments, members who shared in leading the congregation to complete its ministry, trusted colleagues who comprehend the realities, and activities and interests beyond one's ministry provide powerful means of God's presence and support.

A BOOK TO READ

Beth Ann Gaede, ed., *Ending With Hope: A Resource for Closing Congregations* (Bethesda, Md.: Alban Institute, 2002).

CHAPTER 10

A TRAUMA IN CONGREGATION, COMMUNITY, OR NATION

A consultant observes, "Traumatic events happen everywhere. With global media reporting almost instantaneously on unimaginable pain, it seems that traumatic events happen every day. Many flash in our awareness for brief periods, others ooze through our thoughts for years. All have a ripple effect through communities that ride the chaotic waves of grief, anger, sadness and shock." Both crisis and trauma are emotionally charged. The difference between crisis and trauma is that *crisis* is expected in the course of daily life. *Trauma* is the result of an unanticipated and sudden event and always involves significant personal loss, which leaves the individual feeling devastated and out of control. In her book *Congregational Trauma: Caring, Coping, and Learning*, Jill Hudson, a Presbyterian minister and former presbytery official, defines trauma as the large-scale effect of sudden, unexpected crisis even on a large group of people—including the system we call a congregation.[1] While Hudson's work is primarily about trauma within a congregation, much of her guidance will also be useful when broader trauma occurs. Traumatic events are unique. Rather than being stable and easily understood, both the facts and dynamics of a traumatic event change quickly. Some traumatic events are triggered intentionally; others are accidental. People's reactions are more pronounced when a trauma results from an intentional act. Not all information is immediately available in a trauma. Details come in bits and pieces over time.

THE NATURE OF THE TRANSITION

Trauma is initially overwhelming. It permanently changes the environment and the lives of all who live within it. People experience a sense of smallness and feel extremely vulnerable or terrorized. Fear and panic aggravate their pain and loss. Shock, numbness, tears, anger, guilt, and depression are common. God feels far away. People's beliefs about God become unstable as they question how a loving God could allow evil to exist. People often abandon mature beliefs and revert to the beliefs and patterns they learned in childhood or early in their faith development.

For people of faith, a primary task of recovering from trauma is the eventual integration of the absurd reality of what happened into their understanding of life. In the wake of trauma, there appears always to be some period, whether intense or mild, of questioning life's meaning and purpose and wondering if the God in whom we believe has an active role in the world.[2] Biblical answers are inconsistent and unsatisfactory. Scripture reveals four patterns that explain the relationship of God and trauma.[3]

1. We are God's "chosen" people, sometimes chosen to suffer, sometimes chosen to be spared.
2. God makes things happen for a reason.
3. People can influence events and even God.
4. Life is a complicated pattern of growth and change influenced by many interacting factors.

Questioning God is the start of the rebuilding process for most people; the church needs to assure people that God can handle our doubts and questions and, in fact, welcomes them. After much questioning, the concept of God that people end up with may not match the concept of God they held before the traumatic event occurred.

Maintaining a normal routine provides comfort, support, and stability. The healing presence of group members lessens the impact of mass trauma. Healing of individuals is hastened when they remain connected to the courage and healing journey of the entire group. Worship must continue as usual on the Sunday after the incident. Special congregational gatherings for conversation, prayer, support, and fellowship are also essential following a trauma.

HOLY AND ACTIVE LISTENING

In the aftermath of a traumatic event, it is essential that preachers listen to groups within and outside the congregation, to media reports, to victims, family members, witnesses, caregivers, health professionals, security providers, and ordinary people. Preachers listen for people's mood, for their anxiety. They try to determine how people are carrying their emotions and what those emotions are. Preachers listen in order to love people. They do not correct, teach, or even answer their questions. People suffering from trauma are not able to accept any answers. "There is no answer for this!" They cry. Any theological explanations of suffering is totally unsatisfying.

Preachers listen to discover where the congregation stands in this event. As with all change, even the facts of life or death are neutral. Our response to events gives facts a positive or negative meaning. The preacher's task is interpretation, which depends on where the congregation stands in relation to the facts. The pastor therefore seeks to discover who is affected and who is not, the level of the congregation's concern, and the nature and intensity of its reactions. In particular, the pastor will be attuned to the defense mechanisms at work in the congregation. Demonizing, isolation, popular piety, civil or cultural religious expression, anger, revenge, hopelessness, and denial are all ways people seek to protect themselves in the aftermath of trauma. The preacher considers what generations are most traumatized by the event and what age groups are less affected. The preacher discerns how this event alters the congregation's collective memory, whether that memory is irreparably broken, and how God fits into all that the preacher hears.

Preachers consider how healthy the congregation was before the trauma. The healthier the congregation, the more likely it is to survive the aftermath—healthier congregations are better able to handle grief. Congregations have patterns and personalities just as families do. Preachers might ask themselves, "How does this family handle grief? What are the congregation's patterns of managing conflict and dealing with hardship?"[4]

At the same time, congregational grief is hard to assess because people differ in their capacity to respond to trauma. Almost half the members of a congregation will continue to suffer severe traumatic stress symptoms for months after a traumatic event.[5] Preachers are careful not to confuse a few visible people for the entire congregation. Preachers remember that the congregation includes people directly and intimately affected by the event, as well as people who, while more distanced, are shaken by their awareness of their own vulnerability and that of the human community. Remaining attentive to the various stages of grief and healing occurring in the congregation is essential.

BIBLICAL STORIES AND IMAGES

- Habakkuk 1:1-2: This powerful lament to God gives voice to our terror and frustration that, when violence struck, we turned to God for help and God did not respond.
- Mark 15:34: Jesus' cry from the cross gives permission for us to feel and express being forsaken by God as Jesus did.
- Daniel 3: The story of Shadrach, Mesach, and Abednego reminds us that God does not abandon us in our ordeal. Like these servants, we pray that, even if we are not spared, we will not lose faith.
- Jeremiah 8:14-22: Jeremiah says, "We look for peace but find no good, for a time of healing, but there is terror instead." This text expresses feelings of terror and reminds us that we only find true security in God.
- For additional suggestions, see Jeter, *Crisis Preaching*, chapter 7, "Biblical Resources for Crisis Sermons: An Annotated Lectionary." Jeter offers text suggestions and brief commentary for topics including natural disaster, explosions, crashes, collapses of buildings, diseases and epidemics, terrorism, war and rumors of war, assassination and murder, economic upheaval and uncertainty, and tragedies within the faith community.

PREPARING TRANSITIONAL SERMONS

Ideally, people will have already developed an adequate theology for understanding trauma and language for expressing it before trauma strikes. Preaching with a consistent message of God's presence in brokenness, weakness, and the crucified ones lays this foundation and strengthens the congregation to live faithfully, if shakily, with and through traumatic events. Since there is no place for teaching at the moment of trauma, questions of theodicy are best addressed before a traumatic event occurs. Ideally, teaching and preaching on God and suffering occur regularly as the lectionary or sermon series warrants. When prior preaching and pastoral acts have created a bond of trust between the preacher and the congregation, the congregation will look to the church as a place for "safe" grieving. A compassionate church makes it easier for people to imagine God's immense comfort and to offer God the full measure of their emotions and laments.

In the immediate aftermath of trauma, the timing of the event in relation to the sermon and the congregation's psychic and spiritual fragility provides the immediate context for preaching. The goal of preaching in the wake of trauma is to keep open the line of communication between the grieving congregation and God by serving as an intermediary between God and God's people.[6] The preacher brings the people's pain and shock before God. The preacher announces God's presence and purpose to the people and provides them with an interpretation of the event from God. He or she also enacts and encourages communication with God and appropriate responses to the trauma. For the congregation and many others who respond to the trauma by coming to church, no authority besides the preacher fulfills this role.

The preacher verifies for the listeners that the trauma did in fact occur, bringing death with it. The death visited upon the community may include physical and spiritual death, and the loss of identity and beliefs, as well as the loss of the scriptural realities the congregation held as absolute. This is a time for truth telling. Preaching a glossed-over version of reality will alienate listeners and diminish their capacity to see how God is entering into the situation. The issues the congregation and community face can and must be named; to ignore or dismiss them denies the raw honesty of the emotions that are swirling through the community.

In preaching about the reality of the trauma, the pastor decides what information needs to be shared from the pulpit, and why. The need for honesty, confidentiality, discretion, and an acknowledgment of listeners' curiosity helps to determine what will be heard from the pulpit. To determine what information to share, the preacher discerns what the congregation knows and what remains unknown. Learning what information the media are reporting and what information has been suppressed or hidden is essential. *Careful* reporting from the pulpit is absolutely necessary, because what the preacher says will be received as "gospel truth," even if it contains inaccuracies. The pulpit presents a platform of trust that will be enhanced or diminished by the accuracy or inaccuracy of preached "facts." Preaching with informed awareness gives the congregation some "control" over the event. For example, people will be relieved to know that the music director committed suicide and was not murdered. Further, by carefully discerning what information to share, the preacher will eliminate assumptions that may be misguided or false. For example, the school ambush was carried out by outside gangbangers, not by fellow students.

The description of the trauma is not sensational, glossed over, or avoided. Instead, the preacher accompanies the congregation in its pain. In describing the trauma, preachers recognize the limits of language to express what people experience, feel, and believe. Description leads to lamentation—a response to grief and pain that is found throughout the Bible. In keeping with the biblical pattern, the lament of a devastated community is directed to God and leads to the proclamation of the God of compassion who listens, comforts, and weeps with God's people. Lamentation leads to questioning, which keeps our relationship with God alive.

The preacher names people's feelings, admitting that those gathered share a confused set of emotions including anger, disbelief, sadness, fear, disorientation, anxiety, and loneliness. Preachers address people's grief completely, while recognizing that people are at various stages of grieving. Preachers acknowledge the full impact of the trauma, particularly the reality that the event tragically changed the entire community. In responding to people's feelings, the preacher embraces on God's behalf all who are directly and indirectly affected by the event and declares that the event created a traumatized community.

Addressing the people on God's behalf, the preacher provides a context for interpreting the trauma that speaks to and draws upon our relationship with God. In this way, the preacher shapes the congregation's response to the event. As part of this interpretation, she unsentimentally remembers the past, names the destruction of the present, and hopes in the recollected promises of God.[7] She declares that, in many ways, the trauma is a mystery. We will never fully know everything about the event, including why it happened now and why it happened to us. The preacher reminds the congregation of God's promises. Despite the unknowns, we know that God's presence and promises are trustworthy. God's answer to evil is victory, not understanding.[8] On the cross, Jesus entered into evil and trauma. In raising Jesus from the dead, God declared that divine love and life will triumph.

In response to the trauma, the preacher invites the congregation to enter into a state of dependence on God in which the pain of life is released and God's promises are embraced. Such dependence renews and redefines the congregation's identity as people grounded in God's promises rather than as the victims of trauma. This renewed identity empowers the congregation to grieve together; in so doing the members assure one another that God has not abandoned them. The community gathered around God's Word hears and feels God's nearness and presence, even in the story they are struggling to tell. "The hope is not that someday the listeners will become a part of God's story, but that God has broken into ours."[9] When the preacher uses "we" language, the sense of community is reinforced as listeners are empowered to reflect and respond together. By using "we" language, the preacher also avoids drawing a theological line between "us" and "them," which provides a temporary but unsatisfying understanding of the event.

Finally, preachers articulate a vision and identity that acknowledge the participation of the community in God's response to suffering. In leading the congregation's response to the trauma, preachers first publicly ask God to give everyone courage, wisdom, strength, and the faith to be patient. We then empower the congregation to survive by restoring equilibrium, reconnecting people to their coping skills, and making people feel safe. Now we are ready to help the congregation understand how its response witnesses to Christ because, in the face of trauma, the church's mission is to embody the vulnerable, healing, forgiving, transforming power of Christ in the world. A congregational stance of openness and vulnerability exemplifies the healing and forgiving love of Christ in the church's public presence.

In time, the preacher will help the congregation grapple with God's call to forgive. Timing must be carefully considered when preaching forgiveness. Preaching forgiveness too soon will increase people's hostility. Both forgiveness and preaching about it are processes rather than one-time events. Left to ourselves, we may find forgiveness impossible. Only God's patient love slowly brings us to the awareness that forgiveness is our calling, that God is the reason, that God gives to us the ability to forgive, and that healing comes through that ability to forgive. Forgiveness takes time because anger and vengeance are tools of survival. Yet, in response to God, we must begin to forgive. For some, the process of forgiving may not be accomplished in their lifetime.

ANCHORED IN GOD

Before trauma strikes, preachers examine their ability to preach about loss and grief, uncovering the issues that tap into their fears, anxiety, anger, and their own grief and loss. Preachers honestly identify their limitations and what help they need to maintain a ministry of presence with the congregation and community. They also carefully consider their personal theology of suffering, God's will, and evil. Where does the pastor stand in the traumas of war, terror, child abuse, murder and capital punishment? Where does the preacher find God in these circumstances? Do we distinguish between the gospel and optimism? After the reality of loss, do we hope for the restoration of what has been lost or a new beginning through the inseparable love of God? Considering these and other issues in advance of trauma helps make preaching and ministry possible when trauma occurs.

After a traumatic event, clergy may experience delayed stress. By putting their emotions on hold until the crisis is under control, pastors tend to hold up well in the immediate aftermath so they can perform their duties and take care of others—and only later fall apart. Preachers must determine and ask for the care they need to work through their own feelings, both for the sake of their recovery and their preaching and ministry. In the aftermath of some traumas, as when the preacher is directly and intimately affected, he or she should ask that someone else preach at the Sunday (or next) service and longer if necessary.

A BOOK TO READ

Jill M. Hudson, *Congregational Trauma: Caring, Coping, and Learning* (Bethesda, Md.: Alban Institute, 1998).

CHAPTER 11

BETRAYAL OF TRUST

While clergy sexual misconduct, sexual harassment, and child sexual abuse are the most commonly recognized and serious boundary violations within congregations, preachers and congregations dare not equate betrayals of trust within congregations exclusively with these offenses. If pastors and congregations fail to grasp that betrayals of trust occur in ways that have nothing to do with sex, they risk distancing themselves from the possibility that they themselves may become involved in boundary violations.

Betrayals of trust take many forms, including financial impropriety, breach of confidentiality, substance abuse, and misuse of power. Frequent outbursts of anger and a pattern of constantly putting people down are boundary violations. Misuse or theft of funds betrays the trust of everyone who contributed to the church. When clergy are seriously impaired by substance abuse, the congregational dynamics are similar to those of alcoholic families. When they recognize the many forms that betrayals of trust can take, pastors and congregations are empowered to establish healthy boundaries in all aspects of their lives. While this brief highlights betrayals of trust by clergy, boundary violations that seriously damage congregations may involve congregational leaders other than the pastor. One consultant commented, "Boundaries involve more than sex, and violations involve more than clergy."

THE NATURE OF THE TRANSITION

Betrayals of trust in congregations are rarely obvious or easy to discover for several reasons. For information to surface and for congregations to fit the pieces of the puzzle together, parishioners must be willing to "compare notes" on their experience, to document behaviors over time, and to present this documentation to church officials. People must become vulnerable enough to discuss such taboo subjects as sex and money. Uncovering betrayals of trust is further complicated by the congregants' holding varying degrees of secular power based on wealth, position, race, age, class, and gender. Naming who is "powerful" and who is "powerless" becomes problematic. Moreover, some people who bring their own family-of-origin issues into an unhealthy congregation may find themselves comfortable there because the congregation replicates their own family system.

Congregations are dramatically affected when spiritual leaders betray their trust. People expect clergy and other church leaders to be trustworthy in relating to their children and "safe" for all who bring their vulnerabilities to God through the church.[1] The entire congregation goes through a grief process over profound losses, experiencing pain, anger, hurt, and an overwhelming sense of betrayal. Confusion, denial, anger, and chaos reign. People's responses depend on how they view the pastoral office, how close they are to the pastor, and how credible they find the allegations to be. While all violations must be taken seriously, the gravity of violations varies—and therefore so does the congregation's response. When a betrayal of trust is revealed and people recall intense moments of loss or joy when the pastor's presence was a blessing, they can feel as though those profound moments are now turning to ashes.[2]

If a long-ago betrayal of trust was covered up, people will commonly remain troubled and have difficulty working together. Congregations can be plagued by serious conflict or depression for years as a direct result of boundary violations. People may question their faith as they confront this manifestation of sin in their midst. The community most likely has poor interpersonal boundaries because people do not understand how their faith connects to their behavior. They do not comprehend how to relate to one another emotionally, behaviorally, or intellectually in ways that are in keeping with their faith. Pastoral or congregational leadership may change, members may leave, and the structure of the congregation may shift. These are all manifestations of the congregation's inability to trust and function in healthy ways. This scenario is particularly likely if the congregation was not informed about the nature of the betrayal and therefore was never given the opportunity to work together with a professional trained to help the members recover from the betrayal.

In terms of congregational transition, an *ending* occurs when betrayals of trust are alleged, investigated, and brought into the open.[3] When allegations are made, the congregation immediately consults its church judicatory. Judicatory leaders work with the congregation to air their feelings. These officials also explain the investigative process, provide safe ways of reporting issues of abuse, and devise a plan by which the congregation will address the betrayal of trust. While the accusations are being investigated, the congregation is in an excruciating limbo. After the allegations are carefully considered and the victims' accounts are deemed credible, a judgment is made by a fair process. If the allegations are found to be true, safety and justice require truth telling. Congregations that are not told the truth sense nonetheless that something terrible has happened; they imagine violations that might be worse than what actually occurred. Congregations that are "protected" from the truth by church leaders often feel demeaned and patronized. The needs of victims are always primary when decisions are made about disclosure. When vulnerable or easily identifiable victims are still in the congregation, disclosure may not be possible if a victim does not want the case made public. Truth telling should always be done by a church official who is not a member of the congregation, such as a judicatory leader or consultant. People should receive sufficient information so that they understand the scope and duration of the violation and can neither minimize the behavior nor blow it out of proportion in their imaginings. After the disclosure, people need opportunities to express their feelings in small groups, following ground rules that make it safe for people to share. They also need education about the issue. The congregation is encouraged to reflect spiritually on where people find God in this situation, perhaps by naming a Bible story or hymn that speaks to them. Leaders then invite the congregation to participate in planning next steps.

The *liminal strand* is the often lengthy period after the betrayal of trust is disclosed to the congregation.[4] The congregation addresses what it determines to be continuing needs. Typically, leaders provide ways for individuals to express their feelings, create small groups (such as therapy groups for survivors of abuse or a group that prays for the congregation), and offer education on issues related to the situation, such as family-of-origin issues or a study of the congregation's history. Later in this period, follow-up congregational meetings are held. Whether the offender remains in the congregation, it is important for the healing process to acknowledge the offender, even when the congregation cannot address that person directly. For example, the congregation comes to terms with a pastor who has been removed from the congregation by inviting small groups to share their positive, negative, and mixed *first-person-only* experiences of the offending pastor's ministry.[5] (No second- or third-hand accounts, or sheer gossip should be permitted under the group's ground rules.) The congregation also renews its relationship with survivors, whom some blame for the congregation's situation and who increasingly tap into their rage at being victimized. Eventually, the congregation holds a healing service. If the offender was a pedophile, the congregation may feel so violated, guilty, and abandoned by God that it becomes important to use a litany or ritual to reclaim sacred space early in the community's recovery. Otherwise, a ritual and sermon reclaiming God's sacred space is important after people have had the opportunity to work through the trauma and grief of the offense, and when the community has a clear relationship with the offender and victim(s).

A *new beginning* occurs as the congregation assesses and changes those aspects of its culture that permitted a betrayal of trust and an abuse of power.[6] The congregation identifies taboo subjects and considers both the reasons for the taboo and the implications of lifting it. The congregation determines how open or closed it is as a system, finds ways of welcoming and connecting with individuals and institutions that can help it move toward health, and devises ways of assuring accountability. The congregation reviews its history for incidences of clergy burnout and discovers their causes by examining the expectations that clergy and the congregation have of each other. In redefining these expectations, the congregation empowers the laity and sets appropriate boundaries for the pastor so that the congregation's ministry is shared and mutual. The congregation and the pastor also commit to using power in ways that reflect the reign of God.

HOLY AND ACTIVE LISTENING

In addition to listening to the victim(s) and offender as a betrayal of trust is uncovered, and to congregational members as a betrayal of trust is disclosed, the preacher listens in particular for how the betrayal of trust affects the congregation's ministry of God's word read and preached in worship.

For congregations that emphasize the primacy of God's word, a betrayal of trust might more strongly affect their receptivity to and feelings about the preaching event. An offending pastor is not the only preacher affected by a betrayal of trust. The violation affects how the congregation views the pastoral office and whoever fills the pulpit. Preachers who follow an offending pastor in serving a congregation consider whether the members trust them and are able to hear the gospel amid all their questions about pastors.

Successor pastors learn all they can about the offending pastor's preaching. The pulpit has a history and can be abused. Pastors who betray trust may use preaching to abuse the congregation spiritually; they may say in effect, "You're on God's side if you're on my side. If you're against me, you're against God." Offending pastors might use the pulpit to defend themselves by declaring that, like everyone else, they are sinners who need forgiveness. Offending pastors who have a degree of charisma can use their charm to attract victims from the pulpit and then employ, for their own personal gain, the power that comes with "God transference," the tendency of some parishioners to reassign their devotion to and trust in God to the preacher.

Inappropriate self-disclosure in sermons is often an indication of clergy sexual abuse or other boundary violations. These preachers say things like, "My wife and I are having difficult marital problems and I'm struggling with God to bring us together," or "I want to do God's will, but the lay leaders of our faith community are standing in my way. I have prayed to God to change their hearts, and I am weary of their lack of faith in God and in me." Inappropriate self-disclosure is a sign of poor boundaries. When such verbal behavior is accompanied by a display of poor boundaries in other parts of the worship service, the preacher is "grooming" the faith community. Grooming is the process that offenders use to prey on vulnerable parishioners. The offending pastor employs confusing touch, mixed messages, and the power of the pastoral office to remove boundaries that keep parishioners safe. For example, the preacher reveals too much personal information in the sermon and then hugs a parishioner too long when passing the peace, thus suggesting that she is special to him.

BIBLICAL STORIES AND IMAGES

- Exodus 20:12: The commandment to honor parents presents special difficulty for children who are sexually abused by their parents. In response to betrayals of trust, preachers use Scripture cautiously, explain misuses of Scripture, and provide interpretations that are more appropriate or helpful.

- Luke 12:2: "Nothing is covered up that will not be uncovered, and nothing secret that will not become known." Jesus' words bring God's will and coming reign to bear on betrayals of trust.
- Exodus 20:8-11: God's command to keep sabbath is a helpful way of teaching congregations about boundaries. God created heaven and earth in six days, but rested the seventh day. God therefore blessed the sabbath as a boundary of rest for us.
- Exodus 32:1-14: Preachers might use the story of the golden calf to discuss the idolatry of money and financial betrayals of trust.
- 2 Samuel 13:1-22: The story of Tamor raises the issue of incest and the silence in which it is often shrouded.
- Susanna 13:1-63: The story of Susanna speaks directly to clergy sexual abuse.

PREPARING TRANSITIONAL SERMONS

When a pastor is removed for a boundary violation, a recovering congregation craves information about the next preacher. E. Larraine Frampton, an interim pastor who specializes in helping congregations recover from clergy sexual abuse, speculates that people crave such personal information for two reasons. First, the congregation has been groomed by the offending pastor to connect with the preacher and not with the message. Second, congregants want to know who the transitional preacher is to determine if they are safe. The preacher therefore determines ways of using self-disclosure that recognize the faith community's dilemma. Some preachers include a paragraph in the worship bulletin with appropriate personal information.

To care for the community, preachers do not take sides with the offender or the victim. In situations where a leadership void exists, people look for a strong word from the preacher. In speaking that strong word, preachers focus on who God is, and on God's will for the congregation. Since some offending pastors attempt to confuse their personal identity with God's, some parishioners will not have a relationship with God or understand who God is apart from the offending pastor. It takes time to undo this abuse of the pulpit. Though it may be easy and tempting to demonize those who offend, the gospel calls preachers to emphasize the entire congregation's need for God's love and forgiveness. God's love for the congregation "encompasses justice making for victims, healing for perpetrators, and an opportunity for congregations to move from denial to hope, both spiritually and organizationally."[7]

The congregation needs to hear God's promise of resurrection and hope immediately. Ezekiel's vision of the valley of dry bones (37:1-14) provides a poignant image of God's presence and new life. A consultant suggests lifting up "the human, fallen church renewed by God." In time, the congregation needs guidance on faithful behavior. The preacher invites people to pray for one another, to value each member of the community as unique, and to respect that others feel differently about what occurred. The preacher directs the congregation not to engage in gossip or verbal abuse of victims. People are to seek out the appropriate leader, to express their feelings, and to rely on God to see them through. The preacher teaches that boundaries are God's gift to encourage and ensure the proper stewardship of time, space, material, people, and ideas.

Forgiveness, issues related to the betrayal of trust, and justice are themes addressed at a later stage of recovery, when people are not taking sides. Preachers typically wait at least three weeks after disclosure before introducing these topics. To preach forgiveness effectively, the judicatory leaders who disclosed the betrayal of trust distinguish between forgiving someone and holding offenders accountable for their actions. Though we forgive them, such teachers, therapists, doctors, and ministers suffer consequences for professional misconduct. Using psychological diagnosis or forgiveness as a way of relieving ministers of accountability is not appropriate. Accountability demands that we provide justice to victims and make faith communities safe so that the gospel can be heard. When people are not safe, their faith in God is threatened.

Preaching on taboo subjects related to betrayals of trust can be challenging because people often regard the victim as "the problem." For example, in cases of clergy sexual abuse, members of the congregation might view the victim as the seductress who lured the pastor into temptation. While it is important not to take sides, the time comes for people to know about power and the abuse of power. Specifically, congregations must understand that the nature of the pastoral relationship always gives clergy power over them. Preaching justice may also be difficult when people believe that the victim ruined the offender's life. For them, justice often means punishing the victim. In response to this situation, preachers approach justice as it relates to power. These sermons cannot be delivered before people have worked through their feelings.

ANCHORED IN GOD

Preachers set healthy boundaries, find appropriate ways to meet their personal needs so that the likelihood of a boundary violation is diminished, and establish ways of holding themselves accountable to others when any betrayal of trust occurs. When a boundary violation occurs, clergy should be forthright about their role and responsibility.

Those called to preach in the aftermath of a betrayal of trust find appropriate ways to work through their own feelings. Preachers may be angrily confronted by parishioners who, unable to confront the offender, unleash their feelings on the pastoral office. All preachers may be regarded by some of the congregation with suspicion and presumed guilt. Clergy may question the trustworthiness of their vocation and be reluctant to wear signs of their office in public. They may experience profound guilt and regret over their mishandling of knowledge or suspicion of abuse by others and their own past boundary violations. Recalling past boundary violations causes many clergy to experience fear that they will be the subject of a lawsuit or suffer public embarrassment. As they deal with betrayals of trust, clergy may become confused as to what constitutes appropriate boundaries, suspicious of individuals who seek their help, and acutely dissatisfied with their vocation.[8] Finding safe places to express these feelings is essential to maintaining health and well-being.

A BOOK TO READ

Nancy Myer Hopkins, *The Congregational Response to Clergy Betrayals of Trust* (Collegeville, Minn.: Liturgical Press, 1998).

CHAPTER 12

TENSION OR OPPOSITION BETWEEN CHURCH AND SOCIETY

A declaration of war, a school shooting, a city council decision to legalize casino gambling, a court ruling that legalizes the marriage of same-sex couples, a church decision to consecrate an openly gay bishop, and countless other changes can initiate a transition in a congregation's relationship with society. The congregation's understanding of society's identity and values changes. For example, people may decide that our world has turned its back on God, that we no longer live in a "Christian nation," or that our community is no longer a safe place. Increasingly, the congregation concludes that it cannot rely on the culture to reinforce its faith because society holds values and behaves in ways that differ from what the congregation believes. Understanding society in a new way causes a corresponding shift in the congregation's own identity and values. Increasingly, the congregation's new identity and values are estranged from, in tension with, and even opposed to society.

THE NATURE OF THE TRANSITION

The changes that cause a congregation to reassess its relationship with society are local, national, and global in scope. A change in this relationship might result when a congregation examines public policy, as when a social ministry committee uses a government's budget to determine the government's priorities, compares those priorities with the values of its faith, and finds a conflict between the two. Events that surprise people and the response of either the church or society to those events can also lead congregations to reconsider their place in both the greater church and the society.

An *ending* occurs when a change causes the congregation to question or reassess its relationship with society. The ending does not happen when the preacher alone questions or reassesses this relationship, or determines that the congregation should do so. If the ending is not grounded in the congregation, preachers are frequently perceived as politicizing the pulpit and pushing their own agendas. When the congregation questions or reassesses its relationship to society, a period of disorientation results as the congregation's understanding of and assumptions about this relationship are challenged or shaken. Some members will want to deny or minimize the discrepancy; others will advocate biding their time to see how the situation resolves itself. Still other members will want to act vigorously to change society.

In the *liminal strand*, the congregation reinterprets its faith in ways that address the new reality. Some in the congregation protect their worldview by drawing a line between the sacred and the secular, or heaven and earth. They may interpret Jesus' direction to "give to the emperor the things that are the emperor's" (Matt. 22:21) and the separation of church and state as prohibiting the church from commenting on society. They may argue that the church's responsibility is to save souls and that politics has no place in the pulpit. Others will advocate adopting a fortress mentality and withdrawing from society. For them, the congregation should be a refuge, a safe place far removed from the struggles of the world. They may interpret the relationship between God and humanity, and between the church and society in terms of personal salvation and privatized faith. Still others will be roused to an increased concern for justice and will argue that the gospel calls the church to critique society. Some members express this critique in terms of morality and individuals' values; others offer a systemic critique of the greed, instant gratification, and material success that characterize contemporary culture.

The *new beginning* occurs when the congregation determines how to respond to the situation, affirms or redefines its relationship to society, and claims an appropriate identity. The process the congregation uses to redefine its relationship to society influences the new beginning that the congregation makes. Congregations may feel obliged to vote on their response to social issues. Despite our respect for democracy, the ballot box is in reality a poor way to organize theological discourse. When congregations participate in a democratic process, people are necessarily divided into "winners" and "losers." This is not the kind of Christian community that congregations seek to create or encourage. Faithful decision making places a high value on the continued participation of all members of the congregation and welcomes differences as healthy. This outcome is more likely when the congregation grounds its response in Bible study and theological reflection, strives to arrive at consensus, and respects and values those who disagree.

HOLY AND ACTIVE LISTENING

Preachers should give serious thought to how they understand the relationship between church and society generally, and their congregation and its community in particular. In the 21st century, the Christian character of American culture is highly ambiguous at best.[1] The church no longer stands securely at the center of society. Contemporary culture is characterized by a variety of moralities that include historic religions, new forms of religious life, and secular alternatives to religion. Rather than relying on the Christian faith as a guiding force for their lives, many people are only nominally Christian because they have concluded that the church's language and understanding of God, the world, and human life are not relevant to their own lives in a largely secular world. Society's values are supplied by advertising, economics, national security, media, and celebrity rather than by religion. The degree to which these changes exist does vary among communities. For example, in some communities activities for young people directly conflict with Sunday worship, while in others Wednesday evening remains, by common consent, reserved for the local church's prayer meetings, choir rehearsals, business meetings, and other church-sponsored activities.

Preachers listen to discover the level of consensus on an issue in the congregation, the community, and the greater church. Generally, the preacher addresses this kind of transition by listening, comprehending, and giving voice to the various sides of the issue in the congregation, as well as helping the congregation understand and respond to the division between church and society. Preachers also listen for the level of intensity of feelings and responses that surrounds the issue so that they are not misguided by their own perspectives and reactions or surprised by the congregation.

Preachers also determine the congregation's level of resistance to communities of faith participating in the public arena and hearing about public issues from the pulpit. Some people are uncomfortable with the church's venturing into areas of public policy and justice and may think it inappropriate for the church to do so. Preachers might remain patient and understanding by remembering that much of the congregation's resistance to justice making is an understandable, historically long-standing characteristic of many Christian denominations—denominations that in a Christian culture taught that public policy had no place in the pulpit and that social ministry meant caring for those needy ones who "fall through the cracks."

BIBLICAL STORIES AND IMAGES

- Isaiah 49:1-6: God's people are called to be "a light to the nations" so that God might bring salvation to the ends of the earth. Our mission is not to identify with any nation but to be a light to all.
- Luke 12:20-26: Jesus' directive to "Give to the emperor the things that are the emperor's" bids congregations to consider seriously what things belong to God.
- Philippians 3:17-21: Preachers can help congregations understand that being citizens of heaven and enemies of the cross has communal implications, and that the transformation Christ brings is intended for societies as well as individuals.
- Luke 6:20-26: Luke's version of the Beatitudes makes clear that the reign of God turns society upside down.

PREPARING TRANSITIONAL SERMONS

The preacher's task is to stimulate dialogue on the issue that created the transition and to help the congregation consider and either affirm or redefine its relationship with society. The effective preacher remains sensitive to all sides and encourages people to remain in conversation, even though they may differ on an important issue. The preacher helps the congregation understand that the equating of the cross and any human culture is a distortion of the gospel because the reign of God embraces, critiques, and transcends every human society. The preacher also invites the baptized community to understand the differences between participation in God's reign and citizenship in the world, and to grasp that, when confronted by those differences, Christians respond in ways that are faithful to the gospel.

Before attempting to preach about issues that, when considered according to Scripture and the church's teaching, may lead the congregation to conclude that it is in opposition to the greater community, preachers demonstrate genuine care, trust, and love for God's people. In other words, a preacher shows himself or herself to be the congregation's pastor. Preachers understand people before criticizing them, and love people even as they challenge and correct them. Preachers are also careful not to compartmentalize their ministry by, for example, reserving their pastoral selves for one-to-one encounters while hauling hellfire and brimstone into the pulpit.

Congregations are often more receptive to issues of public concern when these issues grow out of the Scripture read in worship than when Scripture is imposed on a public policy issue to justify a stand on that issue. Preachers therefore name matters of public concern in ways that arise naturally from God's word. The realities of our world may necessitate preaching on a specific situation or issue, but effective preachers make clear that to do so is our biblically based response to the gospel and not the preacher's personal agenda. Preachers lift up the realm of God breaking into our lives and our world in the person of Jesus Christ. In response to this good news, preachers lead their communities of faith to consider, corporately as well as individually, how they will in thanks and praise respond to this good news at all levels of their common life. Using images, the preacher describes and nurtures a Christian identity that offers hope in the face of despair and freedom from the powers that govern our society and even our church. Preachers might frame this identity, which is both individual and congregational, as a "homecoming" into the life God intends for us.

As a congregation experiences tension with society, it may be necessary for the preacher to expand the congregation's understanding of what it means to be faithful. In the early centuries of its life, when the church was in tension with society, one's conversion, coming to faith, and becoming Christian involved "change not just of belief but also of belonging and behavior."[2] In a culture that is no longer Christian and that cannot be counted on to form Christians and reinforce their faith, people need to be taught where they belong and how to behave. Preaching therefore encompasses ethics and justice as well as doctrine. The preacher helps people understand that the Christian faith entails more than right thinking or intellectual assent. Faithful Christians anticipate and live in the coming reign of God. By balancing belief, belonging, and behavior, preachers teach people how those who belong to Jesus go about living in the church and in the world.

As part of this instruction, the preacher helps the congregation to evaluate society's narratives and folkways. The congregation will use some, adapt others, and reject still others. The question confronting congregations and preachers is how to draw upon the narratives, images, and technologies of our time to proclaim the good news while at the same time recognizing the power of these tools to cast and reshape the countercultural message of the God whose perfect self-disclosure is Jesus Christ. The early church seems to have asked whether a given practice was life-giving or whether it would lead to bondage.[3]

To address the specific issue that led to the transition, preachers present and engage in dialogue with church teachings or, more often, acknowledge that the church does not hold a clear position on the issue. When the church holds a definite position on an issue, preachers present that position in ways that do not shame people into agreeing. Preachers are extremely careful when naming any single public policy or position on an issue as Christian. The divergence of perspectives in the church makes clear that Christian faith does not lead in a specific ideological direction, if that is taken to mean a fairly detailed blueprint. God's will and our response are rarely that simple. The preacher calls people to discover and discern God's will within the Christian community and helps people to discern their own theological beliefs and the best course of action given those beliefs. Preachers always give people who disagree with the church's position a place to stand.

If preachers share their own feelings, thoughts, and convictions about the issue, they do so honestly and in ways that do not communicate to different-thinking congregants that they are wrong or outside the bounds of God's love. Preachers do not share their personal perspectives from the pulpit to "convince" others of their position, but to help people to come to their own decision using acceptable methods of theological reflection. The preacher stands with the congregation under the word of God, rather than standing with the word of God against the congregation. The preacher and the Bible cannot triangulate against the congregation. If anything, the appropriate stance is for Scripture to address the preacher and the congregation.[4]

To stir conversation in the congregation, preachers embrace difference in the pulpit. A consultant observed that Paul did not say "in the world" there is neither Jew nor Greek, but rather "in Christ" (Gal. 3:28). As long as we are people *in the world*, there will be differences among us. These differences may even be irreconcilable. These differences are not necessarily a failure of community or an indication of unfaithfulness. Our life together will always include people who see our common task differently. When the congregation does not ignore or dismiss these people, their questions, challenges, and different perspectives can help the faith community to examine and account for its theological assumptions and long-cherished prejudices.

One way that preachers embrace difference in the pulpit is by talking about people as if they were talking directly *to* rather than *about* those people. For example, when preaching about gun control, preachers should assume that people on both sides of the issue are present in the congregation, rather than preaching as if the congregation were of one mind and those who disagreed were somewhere outside the church. This approach takes seriously that the congregation is not completely homogenous. It recognizes all people, so that they remain engaged in the conversation. When preachers describe folk on various sides of an issue as "those who" rather than as "some of us who," they set up divisions that kill rather than divisions that give life.

In sermons on issues of public concern, hearers embrace images and stories more readily than concepts or statistics. Nora Tubbs Tisdale, consulting theologian at Fifth Avenue Presbyterian Church in New York, offers four strategies for using stories and images in what she terms "prophetic preaching."[5] First, preachers move from familiar and comfortable stories and images to unfamiliar and uncomfortable stories and images. Second, preachers use the congregation's story or history to forge a future and then to provide an image of that future. Third, preachers tell stories to articulate an opposite viewpoint in a way that is fair, accurate, and believable. The stories are realistic and not based on "straw figures." The preacher then allows the congregation to overhear the preacher openly carrying on a dialogue with that viewpoint. Fourth, preachers use stories to help people to stand in someone else's shoes and see the world through that person's eyes.

Finally, preachers remember that, ultimately, their message is Christ and not the issue; their call is to proclaim the gospel and not to critique society. When a conflict continues for some time, the preacher does not become fixated on it. Referring to the issue from the pulpit from time to time allows the congregation to know that the issue is not being ignored or swept under the rug, while assuring people that the transition is not getting in the way of the congregation's work of sharing the gospel.

ANCHORED IN GOD

Preachers differentiate between their personal views on an issue and the views held by their congregation. Even when pastors and congregations share a common perspective, they may not share convictions with the same level of intensity. Preachers also remind themselves that a congregation's response to a situation is not necessarily a reflection of the preacher's perspective, faithfulness, and effectiveness. Congregations and pastors often hold differing viewpoints on social issues, and factors beyond preaching may ultimately determine where a congregation takes a stand.

Tisdale invites preachers to "take the long view" as they proclaim and anticipate the coming reign of God.[6] Taking the long view reminds the preacher that God acts in God's time and that the divine perspective differs from ours because "a thousand years in your sight are like yesterday when it is past, or like a watch in the night" (Psalm 90:4). God nonetheless brings wholeness, justice, freedom, and life. This perspective helps preachers to remain patient, to be willing to wait because they have hope, and to preach faithfully without either passivity or anger. Taking the long view empowers preachers to trust and witness that small, incremental changes lead to transformation.

A BOOK TO READ

Alan Kreider, *The Change of Conversion and the Origin of Christendom* (Harrisburg, Pa.: Trinity Press International, 1999).

CHAPTER 13

FACTIONS WITHIN THE CONGREGATION

Though related to the issue or issues, change, or transition that occasioned their formation, the emergence of factions in a congregation is an additional change that signals a transition in the level of congregational conflict. Speed Leas, author of *Moving Your Church through Conflict*, describes five levels of church conflict:

1. problems to solve,
2. disagreement,
3. contest,
4. fight/flight, and
5. intractable situations.[1]

When the conflict escalates to a contest, to a win-lose situation, factions often form. A *faction* is a small, dissenting group within a larger one. In most congregations, a faction consists of fewer than 10 people.[2] In fight/flight conflicts, factions attempt to damage one another; when the situation becomes intractable, factions try to destroy each other, metaphorically if not literally.

THE NATURE OF THE TRANSITION

We might best understand this transition in terms of Leas's levels of congregational conflict. The formation of factions within a congregation is a sign that an *ending* has occurred. The congregation is no longer working together to answer the question or address the problem that it faces. In fact, for part of the congregation, this issue becomes secondary as disagreement leads to division and the breakdown of relationships. Winning and claiming power become more important than solving problems and maintaining community. The theological issue is that the congregation's life does not reflect its identity as the body of Christ. The *liminal strand* is the interval of time during which the conflict either escalates or is confined. Without intervention, factionalism will most likely increase and the level of conflict become more intense. Alternatively, the entire congregation undertakes new ways of leading its life and relating to one another to reduce the power that factions hold and to solve the problems the congregation faces. One of two *new beginnings* results. Either the congregation empowers healthy members and embraces healthy ways of living together, or a part of the congregation is destroyed in some way and the winning side consolidates power.

Speed Leas demonstrates that, when the conflict becomes a contest (level 3), the congregation begins encountering five key distortions of thinking that grow worse as the conflict escalates.[3] *Magnification* is thinking that understands the self as more benevolent and the other as more malevolent than is the case. *Dichotomization* is dualistic thinking that sharply divides "us" from "them," right from wrong, fight from flight. *Overgeneralization* is thinking characterized by the words always, never, everybody, and no one. *Assumption* is the belief that one can read the other's mind and motives. *Double standards* are inconsistent norms, rules, and expectations that grant greater opportunity or liberty to one than to another.

At level 4, fight or flight, the factions aim to break relationship. The goal is that one faction must leave. The choice is either to keep on fighting aggressively or to quit the field of battle. Factions attack to cause hurt and humiliation. Factions attack the other's integrity. Defeat is more important than solution.

At level 5, the conflict becomes intractable. Destruction of the enemy is the goal. The ends justify the means. Parties perceive themselves as part of an eternal cause, fighting for universal principles. They feel they cannot stop the fight since the ends are so important. The costs to society, truth, and God are perceived as greater than the costs of defeating others, even through prolonged conflict.

HOLY AND ACTIVE LISTENING

The pastor is almost always an outsider to a congregational system and may misread that system. He or she therefore works hard to understand how the system works. To understand the congregation, the pastor determines the congregation's leadership structure (the way the congregation governs its life), and its relationship style (the way members relate to one another).[4] In analyzing congregations, pastors recognize that congregations, like families, are willing to put up with some behaviors that seem beyond the pale to an outsider.

Rather than attempting to change factions, leaders listen for the ways the entire congregation supports factions; they then address that behavior. Congregations may desire to avoid confrontation and the hard work of fixing the system. As Christian people, the members may feel that they need to please God by being nice. People may clothe their behaviors and agendas in religious language—a tactic that tends to preclude healthy discussion. It is harder to criticize something that people feel "called by God" to do. People sometimes say devastating things "after much prayer and out of Christian love." People may remain silent about unhealthy behavior to protect themselves emotionally, or because their personal reputation is threatened. People may ignore or tolerate a lot to maintain their view that the congregation is a close-knit family. They may choose to placate the dissidents to preserve unity and keep peace. The congregation may regard putting up with some people and their behaviors as the price of staying together. Volunteers may exclude some people from power. Smaller churches may yield power to a few to keep them happy and keep them from walking out. Finally, congregations may tolerate factions as a way of dealing with competing expectations of the church that challenge the status quo.

Preachers listen for the way people talk to and about each other. As factions form and lines of division harden, people stop talking to each other about the issue and start talking to their allies about their adversaries. Language becomes intense. Magnification, dichotomization, overgeneralization, assumptions, and double standards are verbalized. Generalizing and exaggerating are two favorite forms of expression.

In discussions of issues, preachers are alert to people who appear to be building a case against others, shifting responsibility for mistakes, viewing feelings as facts, perceiving memories as present realities, and regarding distant possibilities as likely realities. Preachers take notice when people impose their own "shoulds" on others, expect rapid change, or become stuck in established patterns. People's attributing responsibility for their behavior to an external cause, assuming all responsibility for what happens, practicing perfectionism, and using magical thinking indicate that the congregation is divided.

BIBLICAL STORIES AND IMAGES

- Matthew 18:15-18: Jesus' teaching on church discipline reminds us that we are called to the hard work of resolution. We are to make frequent attempts to make relationships work. Jesus outlines a three-stage process in which the circle gets larger and more public. The purpose of this process is to hear and recognize others' concerns. The goal is reconciliation rather than punishment; the focus is on the person and not the offense or the rules. When separation is necessary, the church remains open to see the excommunicated return and reconcile. Recall how Jesus welcomed tax collectors.
- Acts 15:35-40: The disagreement and subsequent parting of Paul and Barnabas alerts the church to the point at which it is best to let people leave, to encourage them to leave, and to respect their choice to withdraw.
- Proverbs 6:16-19: The Lord hates those who sow discord in a family. Putting God's hatred of discord up front may help put whatever the congregation is fighting for or about into perspective. Regardless of whatever good cause we are fighting for, God hates a situation in which discord reigns over reconciliation.
- 1 Corinthians 1:10: Paul's appeal to the Corinthians in Christ's name to agree, to eliminate divisions, and to be of one purpose reminds us of the goal of congregational decision making.

PREACHING TRANSITIONAL SERMONS

When preaching about division within the congregation, the preacher addresses the entire congregation, not the factions. The gospel rather than any issue is the theme or focus of the sermon. Conflict is not the central message; Christ is.

While the preacher's first instinct might be to use preaching to combat factions by taking sides, this is a dangerous choice for several reasons.[5] First, taking sides from the pulpit creates an unhealthy atmosphere for the whole congregation. Many members may be unaware that anything is wrong. Once the preacher goes public in this way, everyone is aware of the unfortunate situation. Many people experience pain and anxiety because they feel helpless to do anything helpful. People may have doubts about the pastor and the congregation's leaders, even if they did not have doubts before.

Second, taking sides in the pulpit makes the pastor appear weak, especially if he or she reveals deep and intensely personal feelings on the matter. Some will disrespect and ridicule the pastor. While there are proper times and places to share feelings, sharing personal feeling from the pulpit about factions can frighten the congregation. A preacher may be seen by others as devaluing herself or appear unable to control himself, let alone to function effectively as a leader.

Third, taking sides in the pulpit could make the preacher come across as an ogre. Publicly venting one's own indignation is as ineffective as venting personal fears. The effect is that people are afraid of the preacher. Most important, using preaching to combat factions by taking sides violates the essence of Christian preaching. The pulpit is the place to proclaim God's word, not the place to vent emotions or to chastise adversaries. Likewise, prayer is for speaking to God, for bringing our concerns, needs, and thanksgiving to God, not for taking jabs at antagonists.

In the preceding paragraphs, I used the words "adversaries" and "antagonists." In preaching, all such labeling needs to be avoided. It is judgmental and may be self-fulfilling. Labeling reveals the pastor's anxiety and makes it easier for the pastor and congregation to dismiss certain people. More important, labeling people is pastorally irresponsible.

Instead of labeling and blaming factions, the preacher respects everyone and excludes no one. He or she does not triangulate and avoids narrowing the defined conflict to simple cause and effect. Addressing the entire congregation, the preacher gives a clear description of what is happening and what it means. The preacher names the ways the entire congregation, including the pastor, supports division and factions. She or he also recognizes that the entire congregation, including all factions, shares responsibility for the congregation's brokenness, loss, and faithfulness. This confession is followed by assurance of God's grace, will for unity, and gift of the Holy Spirit that brings forgiveness and restoration. The preacher assures the congregation that, with God's help, the situation can be handled.

The preacher then seeks a sense of coherence by proclaiming that, as a response to the gospel, the congregation's actions have meaning and worth. As people of faith, the congregation has some control and influence over how it will proceed and what the outcome will be. The preacher might remind the congregation of its shared values, interests, history, and goals. If divisions run so deep that the faith community's life is threatened, she or he might make clear to the congregation that its survival is at stake.

The preacher than assures the congregation that its leaders comprehend the challenges and have ways of moving toward health, and that an understandable plan is being put into effect to deal with situation. If the conflict is a contest (level 3), the congregation will engage in collaborative problem solving, mutually defining the problem and gaining information, considering various solutions, and choosing one. The congregation's watchword or shibboleth will be compromise and negotiation. The preacher then articulates an understanding of conflict and fair fighting that is congruent with the gospel and issues the ground rules for how the congregation will behave.

When the conflict has escalated to the degree that factions are attempting to drive each other out (level 4), the preacher recognizes the authority of congregational structures over people and declares that the congregation will observe due process in decision making. Everyone will have an opportunity to state his or her position. Those who need to withdraw for a while are given permission and space to do so. The preacher stresses the authority of the congregation's leadership to uphold whatever decisions are made. Again, the preacher lifts up the congregation's common goals, values, and interests.

If the conflict is so extreme that factions are out to "destroy the enemy" (level 5), the congregation will seek firm intervention from an outside party, such as a judicatory. The congregation's leadership takes all charges seriously, and will investigate them and respond appropriately. To do otherwise invites continued agitation. The preacher may find ways to remind the congregation when the issues have been dealt with to prevent factions from returning to questions already settled. Again, she or he identifies both the norms for conflict and any unhealthy practices that need to change. Healthy practices include sharing control of the process, operating under the principle that the common good outweighs individual agendas, and respecting accountability. In naming unhealthy practices, the preacher may need to be specific. Most important, perhaps, the congregation cannot downplay, ignore, or eliminate tension by trading integrity for tranquility.[6]

The tone of the sermon works to reduce the congregation's anxiety. Anxiety adversely affects a community's health. It magnifies differences and decreases the congregation's capacity to manage or tolerate differences. Clarity and objectivity are also diminished. Anxiety can be contagious. Since the preacher's choice of words and demeanor plays a major role in diminishing the congregation's anxiety, he or she seeks to manage personal anxiety in sermon preparation and to be a nonanxious presence in sermon delivery. In crafting the sermon, the preacher *responds* appropriately to the situation but does not *react* to the factions. The sermon delivery is characterized by a calm, relaxed demeanor and voice.

It is vital to combine preaching with coaching, training, and good models of behavior to bring a congregation through conflict in a healthy way. Congregational leaders must empower healthy members. Rather than attempting to change unhealthy members, leaders name unhealthy behavior when it occurs and address irresponsible behavior by enforcing consequences. Leaders must be committed to disabling rumors, gossip, and third-party complaints systematically. They must refuse to pass on and perpetuate secrets and to keep secrets about secrets.

ANCHORED IN GOD

To keep from being trapped in the conflict, preachers have to be clear about their own biases and anxieties in the situation. Preachers guard their hearts. While we all know that there is conflict in the church, conflict in a given congregation surprises its members. Occasionally, the person most surprised is the pastor. Caught off guard by the vehemence of church conflicts, pastors are wounded when they become the focus. Pastors reacting out of their hurt exacerbate the situation. A consultant observed, "When people see the pastor angry, they no longer see the issues. All they see is the pastor fussing." When a pastor's response it clearheaded and skillful, it calms the entire congregational system.

The approach to ministry most appropriate for congregational conflict has been called "differentiated leadership."[7] In their hearts, minds, lives, and ministries, leaders actively differentiate themselves from their congregations and from the conflict. They know their own mind and act on it, especially when their position differs from the congregation's. Leaders know their own stand and realize how intensely they are committed to it. They take nonreactive positions and can articulate their position clearly and calmly. But they do not impose expectations or demands on others, or suggest that others must hold the same position. Self-differentiated leaders do not use the words *must, should,* and *ought,* particularly when preaching. Self-differentiated leaders put more energy into taking charge of themselves than into changing or motivating others to change. Their happiness and contentment rest in themselves. Even when under attack, they find healthy ways of staying connected to the congregation.

Leaders' best behavior may bring out the worst behavior in others. In fact, the more self-differentiated leaders are, the more likely they are to experience sabotage and resistance from congregants. Self-differentiated leaders are not surprised, hurt, or offended at this reaction. Instead, they anticipate sabotage and prepare accordingly. The stronger the preacher's reaction to sabotage, the less self-differentiated the preacher is.

A BOOK TO READ

Arthur Paul Boers, *Never Call Them Jerks: Healthy Responses to Difficult Behaviors* (Bethesda, Md.: Alban Institute, 1999).

NOTES

Preface

1. Fred B. Craddock, *Preaching* (Nashville: Abingdon, 1985), 23, 3.
2. See, for example, Acts 2:4; 4:8.
3. Charles L. Campbell, *The Word Before the Powers: An Ethic of Preaching* (Louisville: Westminster John Knox, 2002), 68-69.
4. David J. Schlafer, *What Makes This Day Different? Preaching Grace on Special Occasions* (Boston: Cowley Publications, 1998), 7-8.

Chapter 1

1. William Bridges, *Managing Transitions: Making the Most of Change,* second edition (Cambridge, Mass.: Perseus Publishing, 2003), 3.
2. Diamuid O'Murchú, *Our World in Transition: Making Sense of a Changing World* (New York: Crossroads Classic, 2000), 9.
3. Joseph R. Jeter, Jr., *Crisis Preaching: Personal and Public* (Nashville: Abingdon, 1998), 13-14.
4. Bridges, *Managing Transitions,* 3.
5. The "neutral zone" is the label used by William Bridges (*Managing Transitions,* 5, 39-56). The concept of *liminality* was applied to the transitions embodied in ritual by the late anthropologist Victor Turner. See Tom F. Driver, *The Magic of Ritual: Our Need for Liberating Rites that Transform Our Lives and Our Communities* (New York: Harper Collins, 1991), 157-162.
6. Driver, *The Magic of Ritual,* 158.

7. Craig A. Satterlee, *Ambrose of Milan's Method of Mystagogical Preaching* (Collegeville, Minn.: Liturgical Press, 2002), 263-264.

8. Craddock, *Preaching*, 201.

9. Walter Brueggemann, *Finally Comes the Poet* (Philadelphia: Fortress, 1989), esp. 79-110.

10. In his book *Border of Death, Valley of Life: Immigrant Journey of Heart and Mind* (Lanham, Md.: Rowman and Littlefield, 2002), Daniel G. Groody tracks the movement of the Mexican immigrant's journey across the U.S. border, a journey in which the toll of suffering cannot be blithely spiritualized away because the immigrant risks his or her very life to undertake this journey. Along the way the immigrant suffers life-threatening thirst, dangerous drops in temperature, and extreme heat. The immigrant risks snakebite and drowning and may well see human bones on the desert floor. The "coyotes" (human traffickers) have told them to stay low to avoid detection by the border patrol. If they survive this transition across the "border of death" into the "valley of life," whether that transition be by way of a fence, canal, river, or desert pass, the transition will entirely alter their identity so that they are known by their kinfolk according to the way they entered the United States—*alambristas* (wire-fence ones), *mojados* (wet ones or "wetbacks"), or *braveros* (wild ones or those who passed through the wild—i.e., the desert). This profoundly physical experience of receiving a new identity is the starting point for the Mexican immigrant's spirituality of transition. I am indebted to S. Patrick Scully for these insights.

11. Ronald J. Allen, *Preaching the Topical Sermon* (Louisville: Westminster John Knox, 1992), 21-22; Jeter, *Crisis Preaching*, 25-26, 38.

12. Walter Brueggemann, *Cadences of Home: Preaching Among Exiles* (Louisville: Westminster John Knox, 1997), 1, 3.

13. Jeter, *Crisis Preaching*, 38-39.

14. Thomas H. Troeger, *Preaching While the Church Is Under Reconstruction: The Visionary Role of Preachers in a Fragmented World* (Nashville: Abingdon, 1999), 15.

15. Ibid., 19.

16. Ibid., 100.

17. Ibid., 105.

18. Campbell, *The Word Before the Powers*, 2-3.

Chapter 2

1. Mark A. Olson, *Moving Beyond Church Growth: An Alternative Vision for Congregations* (Minneapolis: Augsburg Fortress, 2001), 73.
2. Campbell, *The Word Before the Powers*, 73.
3. Olson, *Moving Beyond Church Growth*, 44.
4. Schlafer, *What Makes This Day Different?*, 11-21.
5. Katie Day, *Difficult Conversations* (Bethesda: Alban Institute, 2001), 79.
6. Bridges, *Managing Transitions*, 48-49.
7. Michael P. Nichols and Richard C. Schwartz, *Family Therapy: Concepts and Methods*, fifth edition (Boston: Allyn and Bacon, 2001), 42.
8. African American worship is described as revolving around "preaching, praying, and singing," which together create "an inner experience of assurance, affirmation, courage, and a feeling of empowerment" so that "one experiences oneself as victorious . . . regardless of the external tragic circumstances of life" in Frank A. Thomas, *They Like to Never Quit Praisin' God: Celebration in Preaching* (Cleveland: United Church Press, 1997), 31-32. The Second Vatican Council asserted that "the homily . . . is to be highly esteemed as part of the liturgy itself; in fact, at those Masses which are celebrated with the assistance of the people on Sundays and feasts of obligation, it should not be omitted except for a serious reason," in *The Constitution of the Sacred Liturgy of the Second Vatican Council and the Motu Proprio of Pope Paul VI* (New York: Paulist Press, 1964), 48. *The United Methodist Book of Worship* (Nashville: United Methodist Publishing House, 1993), 13-14, calls for the Sunday service to be a "Service of Word and Table." The Evangelical Lutheran Church in America asserts that "the two principal parts of the liturgy of Holy Communion, the proclamation of the Word of God and the celebration of the sacramental meal, are so intimately connected as to form one act of worship." Evangelical Lutheran Church in America, *The Use of the Means of Grace: A Statement on the Practice of Word and Sacraments* (Minneapolis: Augsburg Fortress, 1997), 38.
9. Satterlee, *Ambrose of Milan's Method*, 295-297; Craig A. Satterlee, *Presiding in the Assembly* (Minneapolis: Augsburg Fortress, 2003), 49-51.
10. Olson, *Moving Beyond Church Growth*, 64.

Chapter 3

1. For this brief discussion of homiletic method, as for many other things, I am indebted to John Allyn Melloh. See "Homily Preparation: A Structural Approach," *Liturgical Ministry* 1 (Winter 1992): 21-26.
2. Barbara Brown Taylor, *The Preaching Life* (Cambridge, Mass.: Cowley Publications, 1993), 80.
3. David Buttrick, *Homiletic: Moves and Structures* (Philadelphia: Fortress, 1987), 405.
4. Brueggemann, *Cadences of Home*, 12.
5. David L. Bartlett, *Between the Bible and the Church: New Methods for Biblical Preaching* (Nashville: Abingdon, 1999), 11.
6. Allen, *Preaching the Topical Sermon*, 3.
7. Ibid.
8. Ibid., ix.
9. Troeger, *Preaching . . . Under Reconstruction*, 100.
10. Ibid.
11. Ibid., 99.
12. Justo L. González and Catherine G. González, *The Liberating Pulpit* (Nashville: Abingdon, 1994), 88-89.
13. Ibid., 81.
14. Ibid., 84.
15. Craddock, *Preaching*, 137-138.
16. Allen, *Preaching the Topical Sermon*, 63.
17. Ibid., 64.
18. David L. Bartlett, *What Is This Good News?* (Louisville: Westminster John Knox, 2003), 2.
19. Troeger, *Preaching . . . Under Reconstruction*, 116.
20. Ibid., 116-117.
21. Bartlett, *What Is This Good News?*, 2.
22. Craddock, *Preaching*, 172.
23. Allen, *Preaching the Topical Sermon*, 73.
24. Craddock, *Preaching*, 171.
25. For a discussion of sermon forms, see, for example, Allen, *Preaching the Topical Sermon*, 75-93; Craddock, *Preaching*, 170-189; Satterlee, *Ambrose of Milan's Method*, 252-259.
26. Brueggemann, *Cadences of Home*, 16-23.

27. Brueggemann, *Cadences of Home,* 16.
28. Ibid., 19.
29. For a fuller discussion of sermon delivery, see Satterlee, *Ambrose of Milan's Method,* 282-304.
30. Walter J. Burghardt, S.J., *Preaching: The Art and the Craft* (New York: Paulist Press, 1987), 117.

Chapter 4

1. This discussion is informed by Jean Stairs, *Listening for the Soul* (Minneapolis: Fortress, 2000), 15-35.
2. Stairs, *Listening for the Soul,* 15.
3. Allen, *Preaching the Topical Sermon,* 42.
4. Buttrick, *Homiletic Moves and Structures,* 408.
5. Bridges, *Managing Transition,* 32.
6. Allen, *Preaching the Topical Sermon,* 52.
7. Buttrick, *Homiletic Moves and Structures,* 408-410.
8. Ibid., 408-410.
9. Allen, *Preaching the Topical Sermon,* 54-55.
10. Ibid., 40-41.

Chapter 5

1. Ronald A. Heifetz and Marty Linsky, *Leadership on the Line: Staying Alive through the Dangers of Leading* (Boston: Harvard School of Business Press, 2002), 30.
2. Ibid., 13. For a complete discussion of adaptive change, see 13-20.
3. Ibid., 30.
4. Ibid., 38.
5. Ibid., 20.
6. Ibid., 2.
7. See Leviticus 16.
8. See Exodus 14:11-12; Numbers 20:4; 21:5.
9. Heifetz and Linsky, *Leadership on the Line,* 93-94.
10. Other examples include Deuteronomy 14:2; Isaiah 41:8-9; and 1 Peter 2:9.

11. John Wesley, *The Works of John Wesley*, third edition, complete and unabridged (Peabody, Mass.: Hendrickson Publishers, 1984), 1:86.
12. Craddock, *Preaching*, 212.
13. See Psalms 36:7; 57:1; 61:4; 63:7.
14. Heifetz and Linsky, *Leadership on the Line*, 188.
15. Ibid., 190.
16. Ibid., 198.
17. Ibid., 184.
18. See Genesis 1:31.
19. Heifetz and Linsky, *Leadership on the Line*, 18.
20. Ibid., 204.
21. See, for example, Matthew 14:13, 23; 17:1; Mark 1:35; 6:46; 9:2; Luke 4:42; 9:28; 10:38; John 6:15; 12:1; 18:1.
22. Heifetz and Linsky, *Leadership on the Line*, 81.
23. Lutheran Church in America, The American Lutheran Church, The Evangelical Lutheran Church of Canada, The Lutheran Church–Missouri Synod, *Lutheran Book of Worship* (Minneapolis: Augsburg, 1978), 153.

Part II

1. Bridges, *Managing Transitions*, 77.
2. Ibid., 84.

Chapter 6

1. Roy M. Oswald, *Running through the Thistles: Terminating a Ministerial Relationship with a Parish* (Washington: Alban Institute, 1978), 3.
2. Roy M. Oswald, *The Pastor as Newcomer* (Washington: Alban Institute, 1977), 1.
3. Ibid., 5.

Chapter 7

1. George Barna, *The Power of Vision: How You Can Capture and Apply God's Vision for Your Ministry* (Ventura, Calif.: Gospel Light Publications, 1992), 28.

2. John P. Kotter, *Leading Change* (Boston: Harvard Business School Press, 1996), 7.
3. People differ about whether the "mission" is the "biggest" entity, with the "vision" providing the specifics, or vice versa. For example, most Alban books use these terms oppositely from the way I use them here.
4. See Part II.
5. Troeger, *Preaching . . . Under Reconstruction*, 129.
6. Barna, *The Power of Vision*, 40-41.
7. Olson, *Moving Beyond Church Growth*, 46-48.
8. Kotter, *Leading Change*, 8-9.
9. Troeger, *Preaching . . . Under Reconstruction*, 139.
10. Ibid., 95.
11. Ibid., 145-146.

Chapter 8

1. In the following discussion, I am greatly indebted to Theodore W. Johnson, "Current Thinking on Size Transitions," and Roy M. Oswald, "How to Minister Effectively in Family, Pastoral, Program, and Corporate Sized Churches," in Beth Ann Gaede, ed., *Size Transitions in Congregations* (Bethesda: Alban Institute, 2001), 3-46.
2. Gaede, *Size Transitions in Congregations,* 36.
3. Ibid., 9.
4. Alice Mann, "What Happens Between Sizes? Why Congregations Get Stuck" in Gaede, ed., *Size Transitions in Congregations,* 55-56.
5. Johnson, "Current Thinking on Size Transitions," 25.
6. Ibid.

Chapter 9

1. Beth Ann Gaede, preface to Gaede, ed., *Ending with Hope: A Resource for Closing Congregations* (Bethesda: Alban Institute, 2002), vii.
2. Ellen Morseth, "Discerning God's Calling," in Gaede, *Ending with Hope*, 4.
3. Ibid., 9-15.
4. Ibid., 10.
5. See chapter 8.

Chapter 10

1. Jill M. Hudson, *Congregational Trauma: Caring, Coping, and Learning* (Bethesda: Alban Institute, 1998), 16.
2. Ibid., 2.
3. Ibid., 2.
4. Ibid., 28.
5. Ibid., 17.
6. Ibid., 11.
7. Mark A. Johnson, "A Bad Day in Hell: Preaching through Grief and Tragedy," *Preaching*, July/Aug. 1998.
8. Hudson, *Congregational Trauma*, 10.
9. Herbert Anderson and Edward Foley, *Mighty Stories, Dangerous Ritual: Weaving Together the Human and Divine* (San Francisco: Jossey-Bass, 1998), 153.

Chapter 11

1. Nancy Myer Hopkins, *The Congregational Response to Clergy Betrayals of Trust* (Collegeville, Minn.: Liturgical Press, 1998), 9.
2. Ibid., 22.
3. Ibid., 37-39.
4. Ibid., 39-43.
5. Ibid., 41.
6. Ibid., 44-48.
7. John D. Vogelsang, "From Denial to Hope: A Systemic Response to Clergy Sexual Abuse," *Journal of Religion and Health*, vol. 32, no. 3 (fall 1993): 207.
8. Kevin McDonough, "The Effects of the Misconduct Crisis on Non-offending Clergy" in Nancy Myer Hopkins and Mark Lasser, eds., *Restoring the Soul of a Church: Healing Congregations Wounded by Clergy Sexual Misconduct* (Collegeville, Minn.: Liturgical Press, 1995), 105.

CHAPTER 12

1. For a more detailed discussion of this perspective, see Satterlee, *Ambrose of Milan's Method*, 312-317.

2. Alan Kreider, *The Change of Conversion and the Origin of Christendom* (Harrisburg, Penn.: Trinity Press International, 1999), xv.
3. Ibid., 101.
4. Nora Tubbs Tisdale, "Prophetic Preaching," Don Wardlaw Lectures, Association of Chicago Theological Schools, Doctor of Ministry in Preaching Program, Chicago, July 6, 2000.
5. Ibid.
6. Ibid.

Chapter 13

1. Speed B. Leas, *Moving Your Church through Conflict* (Washington: Alban Institute, 1985), 17-22.
2. Arthur Paul Boers, *Never Call Them Jerks: Healthy Responses to Difficult Behaviors* (Bethesda, Md.: Alban Institute, 1999), 3.
3. Leas, *Moving Your Church through Conflict*, 20.
4. See chapter 9.
5. Kenneth C. Hough, *Antagonists in the Church: How to Identify and Deal with Destructive Conflict* (Minneapolis: Augsburg, 1988), 146-149.
6. Boers, *Never Call Them Jerks*, 60.
7. Ibid., 94-95.